CW01333149

# MAD LUCAS

# MAD LUCAS

*by*
Richard Whitmore

The strange story of Victorian England's
most famous hermit

NORTH HERTFORDSHIRE DISTRICT COUNCIL

First published 1983
© Copyright Richard Whitmore 1983

All rights reserved. No part of this publication may be reproduced or transmitted in any form or by any means, electronic or mechanical, including photocopy, recording, or any information storage and retrieval system, without prior agreement with the author and joint publisher of this edition, North Hertfordshire District Council. Such agreements to be made in writing.

Typeset by CCC, printed and bound in Great Britain by
William Clowes Limited, Beccles and London.

By the same author
OF UNCOMMON INTEREST
True stories and photographs of ordinary people
and extraordinary events in Victorian
and Edwardian times

VICTORIAN AND EDWARDIAN HERTFORDSHIRE
from old photographs

VICTORIAN AND EDWARDIAN CRIME AND PUNISHMENT
from old photographs

ISBN 0 902755 02 1

# ACKNOWLEDGEMENTS

I am indebted to two doctors without whose interest in The Hermit of Hertfordshire it would not have been possible to complete this book – To Dr Daniel Hack Tuke (1827–95) a pioneer in early psychiatric medicine and President of the Medico-Psychological Association of Great Britain and Ireland, whose 1874 paper *The Hermit of Redcoat's Green* is the only surviving contemporary record of James Lucas's medical history; and to Dr Bernard Mallett, Senior Psychiatrist at The Lister Hospital, Stevenage, in Hertfordshire, who – a century later – has applied modern psychiatric knowledge to identify the precise illness from which the hermit was suffering. Dr Mallett's diagnosis (based on Tuke's paper and other records of the life and conversations of James Lucas) has helped to solve many unanswered questions and, as a result, we can now understand why 'Mad Lucas' behaved the way he did.

I am also grateful to Dr David Parker, of The Dickens House Museum, Doughty Street, London, WC1, for his willing help and advice concerning the hermit's encounter with Charles Dickens; also to the following individuals and organisations for their help during my researches:

The Reference Library of the British Broadcasting Corporation; The British Library Newspaper Library, Colindale, North London; The Honourable David Cobbold, of Knebworth House, Hertfordshire; Mr Noel Farris; The Local History Department, Hertfordshire County Library; Hertfordshire County Record Office; The Library of the Institute of Psychiatry; Mr & Mrs Ben Kitchiner; Mr & Mrs R. P. L. McMurtrie; The Local History and Medical Departments, Marylebone Library; The *North Herts Gazette* Newspaper Group; Mr Stan Piesse of the church of St John-at-Hackney, London E.9; The Public Record Office, Kew; Mr R. B. Williams.

Finally, I am greatly indebted to North Hertfordshire District Council for their generous assistance which has guaranteed the publication of the first edition of this book; to the Council's Museum Services Sub-Committee and their Chairman Phillip MacCormack and, particularly, to the Curator of Hitchin Museum, Alan Fleck, for his advice and considerable help with the preparation of photographs, the editing and publication of '*Mad Lucas*'.

*Richard Whitmore,*      1983
*Hitchin, Hertfordshire*

# REFERENCES

The following books were used as sources of reference: *The Life and Works of Charles Dickens*, by John Forster, edited by J. W. T. Ley (London, 1928); *Charles Dickens: His Tragedy and Triumph*, Vol. II, by Edgar Johnson (New York 1952); *The World of Charles Dickens*, by Angus Wilson, Martin Secker and Warburg Ltd (1970) and Penguin Books (1972); *Out of This World: A collection of hermits and recluses*, by Helen Worden Erskine, John Lane, The Bodley Head Ltd (1954); *Hitchin Worthies* by Reginald L. Hine, George Allen and Unwin Ltd (1932); *The Book of Hitchin*, by Anthony M. Foster, Barracuda Books Ltd (1981).

'Those who come after will, perhaps, have difficulty in believing that such a life as The Hertfordshire Hermit led was not distasteful fiction but a sad, sober fact.'

From the obituary notice of James Lucas, published in *The Hertfordshire Express*, May 1874.

# 1

# INCIDENT AT REDCOAT'S GREEN
(17th April 1874)

To the small group gathered outside his stronghold it had become apparent that the life of Victorian England's most celebrated hermit was ending in anguish. As the pickaxe thudded against the stout oak door at the back of the house the cries of the man inside had reached a pitch that was distressing to the ear. Sweating freely in his thick high-collared uniform of the Hertfordshire Constabulary, John Reynolds was not finding it easy to effect an entrance. The pickaxe had been the only tool to hand and was blunt; the door was thick and the wood very hard—almost as hard as the iron bolts, chains and padlocks that held it secure from the other side. Yet this was still the easiest way into the building, for the occupant had made a remarkably good job of things when he had sealed himself inside a quarter of a century earlier. Across every other door and across every window of this once-elegant country mansion there were fixed great bars of timber. From the smallest window in the butler's pantry to the largest of those that graced the front of the house; every one had nailed or bolted across it as many as six rough-hewn timber baulks, turning what had once been a home of some beauty into an ugly but effective fortification.

Among those witnessing the police assault on Elmwood House were two doctors from the nearby market town of Stevenage and several workmen from the Elmwood estate who were waiting to take a turn with the team trying to break in. There was also a small group of tourists for whom an amusing outing was about to turn decidedly sour. The Mayor of Huntingdon and his wife, Mr and Mrs Bateman Brown – who had come to the area for a rally of Nonconformist Church ministers – had been brought to Elmwood House by their hosts hoping to glimpse or even meet its strange occupant. Like thousands before them they had been lured to Elmwood by the strange stories of '*Mad Lucas*' recounted by Mr Charles Dickens and others in the journals of the day, but now they had arrived they had begun to realise with some apprehension that they were about to witness rather more than they had bargained for.

When the door eventually gave way it took the rescuers some moments to adjust to the incredible sight before them. The room that at one time had been a pleasant oak-panelled kitchen was full of smoke that belched from an ash-choked kitchen range in one corner. The flagstone floor was three feet deep in a vile mixture of cinders, human filth and dozens of mouldy loaves of bread, all of which rose to meet the ceiling in the far corner of the room. Eyes watering from the smoke, senses almost overcome by the stench that issued from the mess beneath him, Inspector Reynolds stepped back briefly into the sunlight and shouted for the two doctors. Each man had only a moment to fill his lungs with fresh air before renewed cries from the far, dark corner of the kitchen drew them inside, scrambling blindly across the carpet of garbage and through the dense festoons of cobwebs that hung, shroud-like, from the ceiling.

The men recalled afterwards that they had noticed his eyes first, bulging brightly but apparently seeing nothing; the eyes of a man racked with pain and fearing death. He was lying naked, shivering and terrified on the bank of cinders, partly covered by the old blanket that had been his only mode of dress since his self-imposed incarceration. One hand was clutching his head, the other stretched out as if trying vainly to fend off those who were coming for him. In a moment it became apparent to the rescuers that – although desperately ill – the hermit was in great fear of those who had come to help him and it was only with difficulty that they half-carried, half-dragged him back across the debris, past the shattered door and out into the April morning. Those who had been waiting outside closed in and stopped short, their faces registering expressions that ran a gamut extending from pity to revulsion. For as he lay there on his old blanket James Lucas Esquire, Lord of the Manor of Redcoat's Green, resembled not a man but a creature. The hair on the head that lolled from side to side was 18 inches long and – like the straggling beard – was matted with filth. His laboured breathing caused beads of sweat to burst through the black incrustation of soot, grease and grime that covered his entire body and the hands that clenched and opened as he struggled weakly with his rescuers resembled more the talons of a bird of prey. The fingernails were three inches long, the toenails only slightly shorter.

One of the party groped his way back into the house to try to find a room that was clean enough to take the hermit for treatment but returned shortly to report that all were in much the same state as the kitchen. From the shambles he had managed to find an old mattress, so they laid the hermit on it while they decided where to take him. Someone suggested the Union Workhouse at Hitchin but Inspector Reynolds wouldn't hear of it. A workhouse was not the place for a man of the Squire's wealth and family background, even if his present condition appeared to qualify him as the lowest of the down-and-outs. So Doctor Hill Smith went across to the Squire's tenant farmer Jacob Chapman, who lived nearby, and a room in the farmhouse was prepared. While the Mayor's wife, Mrs Bateman Brown, used her handkerchief and a bowl of cold water to sponge the dying man's face a farm cart was brought across to Elmwood and the old mattress bearing James Lucas was lifted gently aboard. Inspector Reynolds nursed the hermit on that short journey to the farmhouse – his first journey away from Elmwood House for 25 years, his last alive on this earth.

John Reynolds, destined one day to become Assistant Chief Constable of Hertfordshire, would have many stories to tell at the end of his 50-year career with the police, but this one was the strangest of all. Reynolds had been born in the area and could remember when, as a schoolboy, playground gossip had brought to him the first of the eerie tales about the big house that stood on rising ground midway between the market towns of Hitchin and Stevenage. Of the crazy man who had seized possession of it and spent three months locked inside with the body of his dead mother before the police and clergy broke in and took her away for a decent burial. Later, when Reynolds had completed a short term in the Army, he had joined the local police and seen for himself how Mad Lucas, having failed to turn Elmwood into a tomb for his mother, had successfully transformed the house into a living tomb for himself. However, if by adopting a life, quite literally, of sackcloth and ashes Lucas had hoped to renounce the world, the very opposite had happened. The world had come to him. The clergyman who sought to convert him. The thousands of tramps to whom he gave gin and money. Men, good and bad, whom he sent packing with a blast from his shotgun. One who had tried to kill him. There were the medical men – the most prominent experts on mental illness of the time – who interviewed him and tried to analyse him, and there were the London 'swell mob' who brought their womenfolk out to Hertfordshire for a perverted afternoon of hermit-baiting. There was also Charles Dickens, who attempted to interview him in what turned out to be a verbal cat-and-mouse duel, which caused the great author to return to London and pen a vicious critical portrait of Lucas that succeeded only in attracting even bigger crowds. Finally, there were the children, particularly the little girls, to whom the hermit gave sweets and ginger beer. To them, he was 'The Squire' and, in cases of close friendship, 'Uncle Jimmie'. To the majority he was 'Hermit Lucas' but to those who lived around him he became known as 'Mad Lucas' – 'Mad' because they were convinced he was mad, but also because they felt they needed to set him well apart from the highly-respected members of another Lucas family – devout Quakers – who farmed and brewed beer in the same district of North Hertfordshire and to whom James Lucas was not related. So why had he done it? Why had he chained and bolted and shuttered himself away from his fellow men and yet been prepared to meet and argue with them from behind the safety of his barricades? Like many others, Inspector Reynolds had asked the hermit that question but had never received a clear or satisfactory answer.

As the cart rumbled slowly into the yard towards Jacob Chapman's farmhouse, Reynolds looked down at the unconscious figure beside him and realised that James Lucas would shortly be taking his secret with him to the grave. A man whose behaviour had baffled, amused and disgusted much of Victorian England would leave behind him a host of stories from which, perhaps, someone one day might be able to unravel a thread that would lead to the answer.

# 2

# THE HERMIT BREED

When he decided to seal himself inside his house James Lucas was emulating a comparatively rare human practice that was first identified in Egypt sixteen centuries earlier, when Paul of Thebes and a host of fellow Christians fled into the wilderness of the desert to escape the Roman persecution. They became known as *eremites*, from the Greek word meaning desert. Their plan was to keep the message of Christ alive simply by splitting up, each to lead a life of complete solitude, prayer and physical hardship and – by so doing – preserve their faith. They – in the purest sense of the word – were the true hermits; people who returned to the wilderness to live a life of spiritual thought and physical self-denial which they hoped would atone for the sensuality of the rest of the world. Paul, who started it all, was reputed to be 113 years old when he was found dead, still kneeling at the little altar he had made at the back of his cave. The old man quickly became the hero of eremites (or hermits) and established a fashion among religious sects that was to spread westwards and eastwards from Egypt in the centuries to follow.

By the fourth century one sect in Syria had devised an even more punishing form of religious solitude but one which, like that of Lucas, seemed designed to attract crowds. This was pillar squatting. Those who performed it became known as The Pillar Saints, after Saint Simeon Stylites, whose story is so incredible that it might be dismissed as folk-lore were it not for the fact that it was so well documented by people who knew him personally. Having been dismissed from a monastery for taking self-mortification to its extremes, Simeon was 30 when he was inspired to build himself a pillar. It was only six feet high when he took up his abode on top of it but pillar-building became an obsession with him and in the following ten years he built one that ended up 67 feet high with a platform at the top just six feet wide. With only a railing round the top to protect him and completely exposed to the elements, Simeon lived on top of this pillar for 30 years, never once coming down! All the necessities of life were taken up to him by ladder by his disciples. From his perch he preached eloquent daily sermons; he converted thousands to Christianity and was consulted frequently by the Syrian emperors. Many thought him a miracle worker, so sound was his advice on the problems of the region. How he survived the rigours of the elements on his platform for so long would seem to be a miracle in itself – but survive he did, dying in the year 459 AD at the age of 69. Such was his impact that imitators built a veritable forest of pillars across Asia Minor in the years that followed and there are accurate records of pillar hermits as late as the 16th Century.

In the meantime the hermit spirit spread westwards across to Europe in a less demonstrative form, religious hermits preferring to follow the style of Paul of Thebes by living in caves. By the Middle Ages, many were occupying remote islands, crags and hilltops in the more rugged areas of the British Isles. There were others who chose to build themselves a tiny cell adjoining some church or abbey; men and women who allowed themselves, literally, to be 'walled up' with only a small hole, or *hagioscope*, through which they were fed and which was positioned to enable them to see the altar of the church. Those adopting this style of seclusion became known as *anchorites*, their cell an *anchorage*. Perhaps the most outstanding surviving example of a primitive hermit's home is by the River Coquet, near the Northumberland coast, about a mile up-river from Warkworth Castle. Hewn out of the rockface by successive hermits during the 14th and 15th centuries the hermitage is quite lavish compared with other cells and contains several rooms, including a tiny chapel with a beautifully groined ceiling. These then were the original hermits, devout spiritual men and women who believed firmly that the world would benefit from their self-denial and discipline.

Over the centuries the word hermit – like many others in the English language – has been corrupted to a degree and is now applied to anyone who leads a solitary life for whatever reason. It's those reasons behind a person's decision to opt out of society that can – as in Lucas's case – reveal a fascinating and often dramatic story. Oddly enough, very few books have been written about hermits, but in every one can be found the same series of common factors in the background leading up to the moment of self-entombment. Family feuds, atonement for some crime or gross social misdemeanour, the death of a loved one; in particular the death of a domineering parent. A hermit's weakness is emotional rather than intellectual, for most are highly intelligent. That intelligence, undermined by the emotional weakness, leads them to become highly suspicious of what in their minds is a hostile world and the suspicions in turn create in them the need to be isolated and self-sufficient. However, to be a successful hermit one has also to be wealthy. This is the hypocrisy of the latter day hermit's life. He rejects the world and the trappings of civilisation but hangs on to his money in order to provide himself with the things he needs in his seclusion. Those who share the same insecurities but have no money end up as psychiatric patients in homes, hospitals or mental institutions. The distinguished French psychiatrist Pierre Janet (1859–1947) once remarked: 'If a patient is poor, he is committed to a public hospital as "psychotic"; if he can afford the luxury of a private sanitarium, he is put there with the diagnosis of "neurasthenia"; if he is wealthy enough to be isolated in his own home under the constant watch of nurses and physicians, he is simply an indisposed eccentric.'

Although not prepared to endure the harsh physical discipline of their religious predecessors, more recent hermits have still displayed remarkable stamina – existing on frugal diets and yet remaining healthy and living well beyond middle age. So we find intelligent men and women from wealthy families who are emotionally weak, having been brought up under the wing of a strong father or mother. Suddenly alone and unable to cope with the pressures of everyday life they retire into the place where they feel most secure and surround themselves with mementoes of days past, when life was good and they were happy. These are the common features of the outstanding hermit stories from the 19th and early 20th centuries. Some of the best examples come from America, and New York in particular.

The Collyer brothers lived in Harlem district, members of an immensely wealthy family of shipyard owners. Their mother Susie was a strong character, apparently ostracised by the rest of the family after marrying and then divorcing her first cousin – although the separation was amicable and she had her own fortune. Susie went into semi-seclusion with her two sons but was determined they should progress in the careers they had chosen. Langley Collyer became a gifted pianist who gave concerts at the Carnegie Hall in the early 1900s. His brother Homer became a lawyer. Left alone after Susie's death in the 1920s neither brother felt able to cope with the world outside. They became suspicious of relatives, City Hall officials and everyone else, and promptly barricaded themselves inside their three-storey mansion – where they remained for more than 20 years. Langley occasionally scuttled out after dark to pick up supplies of food, or medicine for his brother Homer who had become severely crippled with rheumatism and was unable to move from his room on the third floor of the mansion. Homer remained in that room for several years but refused to allow a doctor inside to see him. In 1947, after several unsuccessful attempts had been made to contact the brothers in their stronghold, the police decided to break in through the third-floor window of Homer's room and found him there dead behind a barricade; a wispy skeleton weighing only a few stone. Langley Collyer had disappeared. Some days later, having obtained a court order, police and public health officials went in through the front door to begin clearing the mansion – and could hardly believe what they saw.

The whole of the house was an incredible labyrinth of tunnels, made mostly from bales of paper, furniture and tons of rock brought in from the garden at the back. Narrow tunnels through which one had to crawl. One of the policemen just escaped death when a booby trap, constructed as part of the brothers' defence against intruders, sent half a ton of rocks crashing down in front of him. It took workmen 19 days to remove more than 50 tons of debris from the house before reaching the main rooms. Among items removed were 14 pianos! It was only when they reached the core of the intricate maze of tunnels that they found Langley Collyer. He had been dead for a long time, having died of suffocation when he accidentally set off one of his own booby traps and was pinned under a pile of rocks. The rats had eaten a good deal of him but there was sufficient left for the pathologist to decide that Langley had in fact died some weeks before his sick brother Homer who was only a few feet away in the next room. Homer, unable to move and his cries for help muffled by the barricades, had died later – slowly and painfully from starvation.

Until the last few years of their seclusion the Collyers had attracted very little attention because it is far easier to disappear in a large, heavily-populated city than it is in a country district where everyone knows each other's business. New York was, and probably still is, a hive of recluses who have been known to avoid society even by holing up in hotel apartments for years on end. In recent years the most famous of the hotel hermits was Howard Hughes, the millionaire film producer who died in 1976. His obsessive fear of germs in the last years of his life caused him to encapsulate himself in his hotel suite in Acapulco – sealing the doors and windows with tape and covering everything he touched with medicated tissues for fear of infection. Half a century earlier, at the America Hotel in New York, Señora Michaela Romero and her daughter Acacia went into seclusion for a total of more than 30 years for a different reason. Psychiatrists today would call it 'unresolved grief reaction.' The sudden loss of a loved one from which they never recovered. Señora Romero's husband, a wealthy Cuban plantation owner, had brought his wife and daughter to New York in 1924 for a working holiday but died suddenly a few days after they had booked into The America. The distraught widow and daughter refused to let the body be taken away from the penthouse apartment until the manager threatened to call the police.

From that moment on, Señora Romero and Acacia – dressed in black cloaks and mantillas – stayed inside the apartment. Food was left outside each day and none of the staff was allowed inside to clean. They spoke to the manager only on the telephone but always paid their bill regularly by cheque each month. The women even refused to accept changes of bedding. Once, when the plumbing system needed repair they reluctantly allowed a plumber inside but spent the entire time standing with their faces to the wall. This strange ritual lasted 12 years until The America Hotel was closed down. It took the proprietor days of gentle persuasion on the hotel telephone before mother and daughter were prepared to leave, and even then they did not set foot on the street outside. They booked themselves into a similar top-floor apartment at The Ashley Hotel a short distance up the street and reached it by leaving The America through a roof-top trapdoor in the dead of night. Clutching their few treasured belongings they scrambled along the network of narrow catwalks that linked the roof of each building with the next until they reached The Ashley and entered that hotel through a similar trapdoor. Once inside they resumed an identical lifestyle. Their sad predicament was perhaps best illustrated by the way they ordered their food each day. They requested not two but *three* meals at a time – and always with a nightly cigar of the kind the dead husband-and-father had particularly enjoyed.

Of the few hermit stories that have been written, those of the Collyers and the Romeros contain remarkably similar features to that of James Lucas. He, too, was wealthy, intelligent and dominated by a possessive parent whom he adored. It was upon his mother's death that he cocooned himself inside Elmwood House and turned the country mansion into a hermit's cave. Yet, although he dressed and ate like the religious hermits of old he also – in his peculiar way – retained a firm contact with the changing world outside. This is what is so unusual about his story. He was, of all things, a gregarious hermit! A recluse who – from behind his stout barricades – was sometimes prepared to meet and even enjoy arguments and discussions with those who called on him. And many did.

'I daresay you think you see a good deal of the world,' he once told a visiting journalist, 'but I see more of it than you can dream of. I have spoken here with the very highest in the land and the very lowest. They are all as one to me. . . . Last year I had 12,000 visitors and as many as 240 in a single day.' The tourists and the articles attracted entrepreneurs. Postcards and photographs showing the hermit and his house were soon on sale and local traders sold china tea-services bearing his image. Poems were written about him and when he died in 1874 a small local booklet about his life ran to six editions and sold nearly 30,000 copies. With the Victorians' unhealthy fascination for freaks of all kinds it was inevitable that he would attract the crowds. Lucas became a greater curiosity even than Joseph Merrick, the grotesquely deformed 'Elephant Man' who became the rage of

London Society later on in the 1880s. However, unlike Merrick, whose *body* had suffered a cruel trick of Nature, it was a deformity in Lucas's *mind* which turned him into a freak – and that illness was of a kind which almost certainly caused Lucas as much mental torment as Merrick suffered when he first became aware of his hideous appearance. As the physical Elephant Man, Merrick at least was treated with kindness and respect when rescued from the fairground showman by Frederick Treves and given a room in The London Hospital. Lucas the psycho Elephant Man was respected by only a few. The majority stared at him, insulted him and criticised him. Because nobody at that time fully understood the precise nature of his mental illness, nothing positive was done to help him. He was classified as a comical madman, and that was that.

It is now more than 100 years since Lucas died and, apart from occasional brief references in local history books, Britain's most famous hermit has been forgotten. This book sets out to record for the first time the fullest possible account of how James Lucas became the Hermit of Hertfordshire and tries – with the benefit of modern psychiatric knowledge – to find out why he did it.

# 3

# EARLY YEARS – THE FIRST SYMPTOMS
(1813–1838)

Although essentially a Victorian character, James Lucas grew up during the Regency period in the well-feathered nest of a member of the privileged land-owning class, was born while England was still fighting off the threat of French domination in Europe, two years old when Napoleon was finally defeated at Waterloo. During his first 20 years he witnessed that astonishing period of Royal scandal, violence and eventually reform during which – as never before – England was a divided country. Two nations, Rich and Poor. The Lucas family had been on the favourable side of this divide for several generations. They owned estates in Ireland (from which this branch of the family came), in Liverpool, Hertfordshire and Bedfordshire. They made vast fortunes from slavery and the sugar plantations of the West Indies.

At the beginning of the last century much of this wealth passed into the hands of Philip Monoux Lucas, who joined his father James in running the prosperous Liverpool company of Chauncey, Lucas and Lang, shipping sugar, cotton and other commodities from the West Indies, where the Lucases themselves owned several large plantations and hundreds of slaves. As with the merchant port of Bristol, Liverpool's prosperity had been founded on slave trafficking – the merchants shipping cloth from Britain down to the West Coast of Africa where it was bartered for slaves. The slaves were then shipped on the notorious 'middle passage' across to the West Indies where those who had survived the journey were sold to plantation owners or bartered for tobacco, sugar and cotton. This was then brought back on the third leg of the triangle to Britain. Although there is no evidence that the firm of Chauncey, Lucas and Lang was involved in the running of slave ships, Philip Lucas himself is described in various Victorian publications as 'an opulent West India merchant' and 'the owner of large sugar plantations and of a large number of slaves.'

At this time Philip married Sarah Beesley, a member of another wealthy Liverpool family. The couple sailed to the West Indies and lived there for a number of years on the Lucas plantations, returning to England when they discovered their first child was on the way. Their return coincided with the beginning of the collapse of their little empire in the sugar colonies, for in 1807 the British government took its first step towards ending the evils of slavery. Slave trading by British vessels was prohibited and the import of slaves to British colonies forbidden. Although it was to be nearly 20 years before the slaves received emancipation, the Act of 1807 marked the beginning of the end of a long and profitable era for many British sugar planters – Lucas among them. He came out of it – to quote a journal of the day – 'a considerable loser.' By this time, however, the family had re-channelled much of their fortune into a wide range of investments, not least property. In 1806, a year before the Anti-Slavery Act was passed, Philip's father James bought Elmwood House and its estate from The Right Reverend Shute Barrington, Bishop of Durham. The estate of some 260 acres cost Lucas £4,435 and, as well as the mansion, included a farmhouse, several other houses and cottages, 170 acres of farmland and a 40-acre wood. At that time it was known as The Titmore Green Estate – 'Elmwood' was a name introduced by the Lucases later on. Servants were installed, the farm continued to be run by the tenant and the family began to use Elmwood as their country house. All this, of course, was before the hermit was born.

On their return to London Philip and Sarah Lucas took a house in the North London area, probably at Hackney, since this is where most of the family is buried. Their first child, a son christened Philip Monoux after his father, died in infancy in 1811, but they had two daughters, Anna Maria and Harriet by the time James, the subject of this book, was born on 22 December 1813. After James there were two more children – a daughter Emma and a second son George, who was born in 1819. By the time their family was complete, Philip and Sarah had moved from Hackney into the heart of London's society area in Marylebone. In 1817 Philip bought 29 Nottingham Place, just off what is now Marylebone-road. One of a terrace of elegant five-storey town houses, each of which had a small back garden and servants' quarters and stables facing onto a mews at the rear. This was to be their home for nearly 20 years – a pleasant spot almost adjoining the parish church of St Mary-le-bone and just across the road from Regent's Park, where the Prince Regent himself was supervising the construction of the famous Regent's Park terraces.

Today, George the Prince Regent is remembered for one redeeming virtue that – as probably the greatest patron of the arts ever to sit on the Throne of England – he provided the inspiration for such places as Regent's Park, Trafalgar Square, The National Gallery and Brighton Pavilion. However, the time at which he inspired all this was a time when England could least afford it. While the Rich ensured they had more than sufficient to survive, the Poor were being slowly throttled by the combined economic strictures of low wages and high war-time prices. The monarch's squandering of public money didn't exactly endear him to his subjects. At this time the prestige of the Crown was about as low as it has ever been. While cartoonists lampooned him with vicious satirical drawings, the Prince sailed on at the helm of a social pleasure boat aboard which the Rich indulged themselves in pleasures, extravagances and debauchery of a scale that almost defies description. London was rife with gossip of scandals and corruption among the aristocracy. On the fringe of all this the Lucas family were probably as disgusted as most for – although strong Tories and of substantial wealth – they belonged to that slightly lower stratum of the well-to-do who had to run efficient businesses in order to maintain their standard of living. Father and Mother would have been appalled by the Prince Regent's gluttony (18-course banquets of 116 different dishes), by his womanising and his gambling. Yet, in 1821, when James was eight, the family would have been among the thousands who lined the route to Westminster Abbey to see the Prince's coronation, which cost a quarter of a million pounds to stage and was breathtaking to behold. Only later, when he grew up, would James have been told about the touch of sickly farce behind the great event. How the new king's estranged wife – the fat, brassy and foul-mouthed Caroline of Brunswick – returned home from Italy after seven years of living in sin with a low-born Italian named Bergami to demand her rightful place on the throne as Queen of England. How she had to endure a public investigation into her morals by the House of Lords and how, on Coronation Day, she suffered the final public humiliation of having the doors of Westminster Abbey slammed in her face by the ushers. When the King died James Lucas was 17 and quite likely read for himself in *The Times* newspaper's unflattering obituary that 'there was never an individual less regretted by his fellow creatures than this deceased king'. These ignominious royal scandals were to have a profound effect on the young man and were probably responsible for one of the many strange quirks for which he became well-known in his later years as a hermit – his declared and absolute hatred for Queen Victoria and all those who had preceded her in the House of Hanover. But that was 30 years away.

For the Lucas family in the early 1820s, Elmwood House was Grandpapa's country retreat. Set in deepest rural Hertfordshire, it was permanently staffed by servants and estate workers and could be reached from London by what, in summertime, would be an enjoyable 30-mile carriage ride along the old Great North Road. The route passed through Barnet, then along by the home of the Salisbury family at Hatfield, eventually reaching Stevenage – which was then a modest market town of 1,500 inhabitants. Most lived in cottages and inns that stretched along each side of the trunk road for a distance of two miles; a community that made a modest living from agriculture and the busy stagecoach route that passed along the centre of their little town. A mile or two north of Stevenage the Lucas's carriage, bearing the family coat-of-arms upon its doors, would turn off the main coach route and sweep into the dainty network of high-banked lanes that teemed with wild flowers. A sharp left turn at the village of Wymondley, a brisk trot up a gentle hill for the last few hundred yards and there, dominating the hamlet of Redcoat's Green, stood Elmwood.

Details of the hermit's youth are not easy to find, principally because his branch of the Lucas family tree has now withered and dropped off. Neither James nor his younger brother George married, and of the three sisters, one died childless and the other two had nothing more to do with their brother once he had embarked upon his hermit's life. A great deal of potential evidence was lost as Elmwood House and its contents deteriorated during the 25 years that James occupied it and after his death George and Emma, the surviving brother and sister, were reluctant to talk publicly about him. So, much of the evidence that has survived is based only on stories passed down through families living in the vicinity of the Elmwood hermitage. Stories that have, inevitably, become somewhat distorted with the passing of time. However, one vitally important and accurate record does remain. It was made in 1874 shortly after the hermit's death by Doctor Daniel Hack Tuke, one of Victorian England's most progressive and enlightened experts on mental illness.

A member of the great Quaker family which played an important part in setting up the York Retreat for the Mentally Ill with the Society of Friends, he became a consultant physician on mental diseases in London. In 1858, with a colleague, he produced a classic work on mental illness '*A Manual on Psychological Medicine*' which was for many years a standard reference. Part of the volume – relating to lunacy law and the classification of insanity – showed that Tuke had begun a new era in the scientific study of insanity. He became interested in Lucas during visits to Hitchin, three miles north of Redcoat's Green, to see his older brother James Hack Tuke, the wealthy philanthropist and philosopher who was a partner in a Hitchin bank. Daniel met and conversed with the hermit and, after Lucas had died, his great reputation for work among the mentally ill gave him easy access to members of the family, who confided in him details which they would not otherwise have made public. Dr Tuke presented the facts in a report to the Annual General Meeting of the Medico-Psychological Association in London in August 1874. The Association – of which Doctor Tuke later became President – retained a record of the report which today is still preserved in the library of the Institute of Psychiatry.

Tuke reveals first of all that there was a history of eccentricity if not insanity in the family. 'It is stated in the newspaper and I find it to be correct, that an aunt (Philip Lucas's sister) was as eccentric as Lucas, and exhibited a like contempt for the ordinary decencies of life. A gentleman (not a relative) informs me that he knew one of her brothers who was also very eccentric, though not in an asylum', he says. As a boy Lucas was considered healthy in mind and body but was indulgently treated by both parents. 'He was in short a spoilt child, getting his own way in almost everything,' Dr Tuke reports, 'and I may observe here that of the patients admitted into the York Retreat it is striking how many were unduly indulged when children.'

So for the first ten years of his life James was a normal healthy child, though dreadfully spoilt by his parents. Quite understandable when one remembers that James had replaced Philip and Sarah's first-born son, lost in infancy at the age of five months. So when did things start to go wrong for him? According to Sarah it was in 1823 when the boy contracted a particularly virulent form of ringworm – or *tinea capitis* – a disease of the scalp in which fungus attacks the roots of the hair, causing inflammation and severe scabbing. 'James,' she once said, 'was never quite the same after the ringworm was repelled.'

An instinctive reaction to this remark is that a skin ailment – then quite common among small boys – can hardly be blamed for affecting the mind of the sufferer; that Sarah had needed to find an excuse for her son's eccentric behaviour in later life and the ringworm was the only thing she could think of to blame. The remark was sufficient to interest Daniel Hack Tuke, who also discovered from a relative that the boy's head had been shaved at the time of the illness and 'a very strong ointment rubbed in'. Tuke made a number of superficial inquiries among colleagues to try to discover whether they had knowledge of patients' mental attitudes being affected by local applications to the scalp – one said he had not but the second, Doctor Russell Reynolds, reported that he had had patients suffering from disorder of the emotions after using certain hair-dyes. Tuke, who made these inquiries some 50 years after James had suffered the illness, appears to have pursued this line of inquiry no further. However, one glance through some of the standard medical books of the 1820s raises the firm probability that it was not the ringworm itself that turned the little boy's mind, but the awful traumas he experienced at the hands of the physicians while – to use his mother's expression – it was being 'repelled'.

1823 was just three years after the death of King George III who – when he suffered a

## Early Years – The First Symptoms

mental breakdown some 30 years earlier – received appalling treatment from his doctors. Led by the Royal Surgeon Francis Willis, they believed then that madness was an evil and that the only way to cure it was by punishing the body of the afflicted man. Mustard plasters were strapped on the king's legs to cause severe blistering which – the surgeons thought – would draw out the evil humours. When in his great pain the king tried to tear the scalding plasters from his legs he was put into a straight-jacket for as long as 24 hours at a time. Although it was 30 years after this episode that James Lucas contracted ringworm medical knowledge had progressed but little. Doctors still believed that many illnesses could be cured by bleeding the patient or making 'issues' and 'setons' – that's to say, deliberately making a wound and keeping it open to ooze pus under the mistaken impression that the pus was badness leaving the body rather than the body fighting to heal the wound they had inflicted.

Bartholomew Parr, Senior Physician at the Devon and Exeter Hospital, described the best way to make a seton in *The London Medical Dictionary* of 1809: 'This operation is performed by raising the skin with finger and thumb while an assistant does the same an inch or two distant, and having armed a large broad crooked cutting needle, made for the purpose, with the necessary number of threads pass the needle through the stretched skin and bring the threads a little way through. They are left in the wound and as much of the thread as will pass through the seton at each dressing must be rubbed with the unguentum resinae flavae, moved forward every morning and evening and thus the discharge will be promoted and continued at pleasure'. One does not need reminding that there were at this time no anaesthetics!

On recommended treatment for ringworm, Doctor Parr continues: 'Authors of credit have recommended blisters, issues, setons either as part of the treatment or to prevent a relapse ... The only effectual remedy is by pulling out the hair by the roots, or destroying these by acrid (bitter, hot or stinging) applications. The pitch cap produces this with much pain and we have known each separate hair eradicated by tweezers. The head also has been shaved and covered with an oilskin cap, which keeps up a violent and continued perspiration, so as more gradually to destroy the bulbs.' In the *Oxford English Dictionary* (1980) the pitch cap has two definitions: 'a plaster containing pitch used as a means of destroying hair on the scalp in cases of ringworm' and 'a cap lined with pitch that was used as an instrument of torture by soldiers during the Irish Rebellion of 1798.'

In a slightly later medical book *'Domestic Medicine or a Treatise on the Prevention and Cure of Disease'*, published in 1820, a Scottish surgeon William Buchan confesses: 'The most obstinate of all eruptions incident to children are the *tinea capitis*, or scabbed head and chilblains. The scabbed head is often exceedingly difficult to cure, and sometimes indeed the cure proves worse than the disease. I have frequently known children seized with internal disorders, of which they died, soon after their scabbed heads had been healed by the application of drying medicines. The cure ought always first to be attempted by keeping the head very clean, cutting off the hair, combing and brushing away scabs etc. If this is not sufficient, let the head be shaved once a week, washed daily with yellow soap, and gently anointed with a liniment made of train oil (an oil obtained from boiling the blubber of whales and other fish) eight ounces; red precipitate, in fine powder, one dram. And if there be proud flesh, it should be touched with a bit of blue vitriol (sulphuric acid), or sprinkled with a little burnt alum. To prevent any bad consequences from stopping the discharge, it would be proper, especially in children of a gross habit (fat children, presumably) to make an issue in the neck or arm, which may be kept open till the patient becomes more strong and the constitution be somewhat mended.' On the subject of making issues Dr Buchan recommends: 'Issues may be made in any part of the body but they generally have the best effect near the spine. The discharge may be greatly promoted by dressing them with the mild blistering ointment and keeping what are commonly called orrice-pease in them.'

Extracts providing ample evidence that up to and including the 1820s a child victim of ringworm was doomed, at best, to endure several weeks of extreme discomfort, weakened further by wounds deliberately inflicted and irritated or, at worst, periods of excruciating pain caused by the use of scalding plasters, acid and other hot applications while the hair was pulled out methodically by the roots. In the 1980s – when ringworm can be quickly cured with antibiotics and fungicidal cream – the consequences of catching the disease in 1823 hardly bear thinking about. One way or another the effect of this kind of treatment on a boy of ten must have been devastating; particularly a boy in a family with a history of mental instability, a boy who had been spoilt and pampered by his parents but who, in his illness, were condoning the frightening and painful treatment he received. If this was not responsible for turning his mind it is a remarkable coincidence that once well enough to return to school at Clapham he immediately embarked on the course of anti-social behaviour that was to remain with him for the rest of his life.

From that moment on he refused to let anyone cut his hair and for four years engaged in a battle of willpower with his teachers. He continually played truant and when at school refused to co-operate in lessons he did not like, Eventually, the headmaster of the Clapham school felt he could cope no more, and James' parents were asked to remove him. The boy was transferred to another school at Richmond, but his stay there was even shorter. In some desperation Philip Lucas sought to find a tutor who would give their son individual attention. He still hoped that someone somewhere could be found not only to cure James of his anti-social behaviour but also to teach him a worthwhile profession. The boy was bright and well-versed in Latin and Greek and liked the Sciences. Perhaps the medical profession? So, at the age of 15 James was sent to live with Dr Hicks, a medical practitioner living not far from Redcoat's Green in the village of Whitwell. Dr Hicks – engaged to teach James 'moral restraint and discipline' as well as medicine – clearly found this arrogant teenager an unpleasant little brat. Years later when the hermit died, the good doctor was still alive and recalled immediately the problem child of 45 years earlier. 'I regarded him as the victim of ill-judged indulgence and injudicious treatment,' he told Daniel Hack Tuke, 'The chief characteristics at that time were incorrigible perverseness and obstinacy, combined with a certain degree of cunning.' Dr Hicks had been given no medical history of the boy at the time, although his parents confided that they were worried by a habit he had developed. 'When driven out for an airing to some common or green in the neighbourhood of London, and taken from the carriage for a walk, he would stand still and shut his eyes,' the doctor remembered. He endeavoured to teach James something of the basic rudiments of medicine but the engagement was a short one. When Dr Hicks was out one day and the youth had been left under the supervision of an assistant, he 'walked off'. The relative with whom he sought refuge refused to give him up – and that was the last Dr Hicks heard of James Lucas until thirty years later when Charles Dickens brought him national fame.

Having failed to interest his wayward son in Medicine, the only other possible vocation Philip Lucas could think of was the Church. Two maiden aunts, sisters of Philip Lucas, who lived at Wilstead in Bedfordshire, found a clergyman in the county town who was willing to undertake the task at which Dr Hicks had failed, but the good parson met with even less success. Having been dumped at Bedford, James once more adopted his ostrich pose, lapsing into silence, sitting before his frustrated tutor for hours with eyes firmly closed. Once again, after a few fruitless weeks, the project was abandoned and James returned to Elmwood, boasting later: 'During the whole of my time at Bedford I never once opened a book.' It's significant that nowhere is there evidence that Philip and Sarah Lucas gave any support to the people they employed to try to put their son on the right path. If the boy ran home saying he didn't like it where he was, never once did the father kick his backside and make him go back. 'His father,' says Tuke, 'was totally unable to manage him; he was self-willed, obstinate and impatient of all restraint. When thwarted in any of his wishes he took offence and would shut himself up in his bedroom, sulking there for days together; indeed he seems to have spent a large portion of his time in there.'

Again, Philip and Sarah Lucas pandered to their son's wishes, and no attempt was made to get him out of his room. At least while he was there the rest of the family could continue its life without having to endure his disruptive influence. Dr Tuke recalls two other interesting facts which confirm that – although only 16 – James was already showing the classic symptoms of a recluse. During his self-imposed exile in the bedroom the boy still managed to maintain a hearty appetite. 'Meals were taken to him and left at his door,' the doctor says. 'He did not object to eat but resolutely refused to return the plates. At length the plates and dishes became scarce in other parts of the household, as his bedroom contained nearly the whole supply in the way of crockery! He would not, I may here add, allow the cinders to be removed from the grate of his room, and the family were in frequent fear lest the house should be set on fire. On one occasion when his parents were from home, and his sister was left in charge, she became greatly alarmed and they were hastily summoned home.'

By this time, too, James was beginning to display remarkable eccentricities in his choice of clothes. 'He would dress by fits in the most opposite manner, sometimes having scarcely anything on, and at others wearing clothes of the best material, and appearing quite the fop,' says Tuke in his report. Having refused to have his hair cut since the ringworm it now, after six years, grew halfway down his back. When he consented to appear in public it would be carefully done up in paper curlers. Small wonder that to avoid the gazes and the gossips in busy Marylebone the Lucases shipped their son out to rural Hertfordshire whenever possible. However, if James' taste in clothes could be exotic, his choice of friends was not and, as he became more difficult to control, he chose to spend his time in Hertfordshire – to quote the discreet Dr Tuke – 'in low company'. Again, an early indication of his preference when a hermit for the company of tramps as much as people of his own class. So James was returned to Nottingham Place and 'an attendant' was employed to look after him. This infuriated him so much that he became even more aggressive and made life so unbearable for everyone concerned that the man was paid off after only a few weeks.

The paper which Dr Tuke presented to members of the Medico-Psychological Association in 1874 is valuable in that it provides the only positive information about the early life of Lucas, as recalled by his brother and sister. In one respect it could be misleading in that it deals only with the negative, problematical side of the young man's development. For there's no doubt he had his good points as well, and the large amount of money that Philip Monoux Lucas spent on his wayward son's education (the hermit later claimed it was £300 a year) was not entirely wasted. James' bad behaviour came in phases and was directed against those who tried to make him do something he did not want to do. The things he enjoyed doing, he did well, and there is ample evidence that those who taught him the basic sciences, classics and sport at the schools in Clapham and Richmond had not wasted their time. He was well-versed in Shakespeare and the standard works of the 17th and 18th centuries; he could read and speak Greek and Latin and he was a keen athlete. In the 1820s sport was considered an important part of the school curriculum for young men of wealth. The popular idea of a gentleman was a man who was a fighting sportsman, willing if necessary to defend his honour with his fists or in a duel. Thus the principal upper-class sports taught at private schools were shooting and fencing, and Philip Lucas ensured that both his sons were educated in this tradition. Even during periods when not at school James received lessons in fencing, drill and riding from a visiting Drill Master and, by all accounts, became something of an expert.

Physically, he seems to have been an attractive young man. Those who remembered him from his early visits to Elmwood in the 1820s and 30s had quite nice things to say: 'He had an intellectual cast of countenance, well-formed features and a gentlemanly manner of bearing. . . . He was below average height but a broad chest and well-developed muscles showed that he was possessed of considerable physical strength. . . . He was a nice young man, rather quiet. . . . Before he secluded himself he was by no means unmindful of his outward appearance, and he used to be as well and as smartly dressed as any man in the neighbourhood.'

So, between the outbursts of eccentricity and bad behaviour, life at Elmwood and Nottingham Place was able to proceed in a normal way with good times as well as bad. James' two older sisters were courted by young men from aristocratic European families. Anna Maria married an Austrian, Joseph Ferdinand, Count de Taaffe, whose family held high posts in the Austrian army; her sister Harriet became the wife of a Polish Count and is believed to have returned with him to Poland.

Father, meanwhile, had busied himself with a new enterprise – helping to finance and develop one of the first major companies to bring gas supplies to Georgian London. In 1821 he became a shareholder and proprietor of the Imperial Gas Company, which installed the first forms of gas lighting and heating to streets, homes and factories in large areas of North, East and West London. Six years after its formation the gas company became the subject of a scandal, exposed in *The Times*, after several of the directors had been discovered to have put their hands into the till. When the news broke some disappeared abroad, to be accused in their absence of appropriating £12,750 of company funds and covering their tracks by putting false entries in the Imperial's accounts books. In the upheaval that followed, the company's rules were changed and Philip Lucas was appointed Governor with the task of restoring its good name. He spent three years putting things straight, during which time – old company records state – 'The Imperial, under the guidance of Lucas, became an excellent employer.'

No doubt the hermit's father would have remained at the head of the company for several years more but in November 1830, at the comparatively early age of 52, he was taken ill and died. Philip Monoux Lucas was buried in the family vault in the graveyard of St John-at-Hackney beside the first-born son to whom he had given his name nearly 20 years earlier. In keeping with the tradition among wealthy families of the time, his widow commissioned an ornate tribute to her husband – a marble tablet, placed on the wall of the staircase inside the church and bearing the script: 'This monument is erected by his widow, Sarah Lucas, under an impression of sincere and fervent gratitude, for the favour of Almighty God in having granted to her a husband, a friend, a protector and counsellor, singularly affectionate, faithful, able and upright; while she treasures as her chief honour, that he was earnestly beloved and respected by his many friends for all good qualities of a good man and a good Christian.' Beneath was an escutcheon of pretence – the Lucas coat-of-arms and those of her own family, Beesley – and the motto 'Quid Verum Atque Decens' – 'Whatever is True and Honourable.'

During the next year while Philip's affairs were sorted out by his executors, his widow had to make up her mind what to do with her family. Emma and George, the two younger children aged 12 and 10, were still at school and Anna Maria, the newly-married daughter, lived close by. So Sarah decided to stay at Nottingham Place for the time being, and the house remained recorded in her name until 1838 when, presumably, Emma and George had completed their schooling. The grandfather James Lucas outlived his son by three years, dying in 1833. Having no other son to inherit his estate he left his Hertfordshire land in trust with Sarah to his five grandchildren for them to inherit on their mother's death. Why, in 1838, Sarah Lucas should decide to sell the house that had been their London home for more than 20 years one can only guess. So large was the family fortune that she is unlikely to have had to sell it for financial reasons. Was James the cause? With his father and grandfather gone he was – as the elder son – head of the family, and Dr Tuke records that at this time in his life his conduct became unbearable. So much so that Sarah – for the first time – called in a Dr Sutherland who issued medical certificates to the effect that James was of unsound mind and should have an attendant with him day and night. A male nurse was engaged, 29 Nottingham Place was sold, and Sarah took James, Emma and George out to Hertfordshire to make Elmwood their permanent home.

# 4

# ECCENTRICITIES AT ELMWOOD
(1839–1850)

Sarah's decision to move away from London for good was taken more to protect the family's black sheep than to hide him. Having acknowledged, at last, that her son was 'mad' she did what she considered best for him. To her, committing James to a Lunatic Asylum was out of the question for, as with prisons and hospitals, the great reforms achieved by the Victorians were still a long way off. Daniel Hack Tuke, for instance, was still at school. In the 1830s an asylum was a place where lunatics were restrained – not treated; a House of Bedlam into which the public were often admitted to enjoy a couple of hours of perverted amusement from the antics of the mentally tormented. At Elmwood, with a medical attendant to watch over him, James would be safe from this – controlled during his disturbed periods but able to enjoy a healthy and happy life when well.

Up to this time Elmwood House and its new occupants would have attracted little attention from the few dozen people who lived in the area of Redcoat's Green. For most people in North Hertfordshire at that time it was one of those rather fine country properties owned by a rich London family, which folk on a Sunday afternoon outing on foot or by carriage might pause at briefly to admire before moving on. Not as grandiose as some in the county, but a substantial country mansion nevertheless – sitting on high ground above the village of Wymondley, with splendid views across the rolling Hertfordshire countryside. Built mainly of red brick, it had several large reception rooms and an additional section at the rear which contained the servants' quarters and kitchen. A gravel coach-drive curved past trim lawns, sweeping by the front of the house to stables and a coach house at the rear. Behind these was a large kitchen garden, and to the front and side of the house were several acres of parkland and a large pond with an island. The property was surprisingly close to a fairly busy lane, linking the village of St Ippolyts, to the North, with Fisher's Green and Stevenage to the South – which is why in later years the public found it so easy to get access to the hermit in his cell. At this time, though, ornamental railings and thick shrubbery afforded privacy from passers-by.

Inevitably it was not long before James began to be noticed. Free from the constrictions of city life he took up his favourite sports with renewed gusto. The drill instructor whom Philip Lucas had employed ten years earlier to train his sons in the athletic skills was engaged to come to Elmwood and in the summer months could be seen putting the Young Master through his paces in the parkland meadow. Riding, fencing, single-stick combat – all observed with great interest by the locals on the other side of the hedge. Interest that might have waned after a while had it not been for the apparel the pupil insisted upon wearing, for it hardly conformed with the standard dress of the young Victorian gentleman. Most of the time James preferred to wear a yellow nankeen (Chinese cotton) suit and no shoes, and the horse he rode – a young mare named Junie of which he was passionately fond – had to suffer similar unconventional attire. Her bridle and stirrups were improvised from rope, and Lucas sat astride her on an old-fashioned military saddle with a cord tied to each peak fore and after and wound several times round his waist to prevent him falling off. A pair of riding boots was slung across Junie's neck should the rider decide he needed them when he dismounted.

All this took place under the constant supervision of the medical attendant. His job could not have been an easy one for he was dealing not with a simpleton but a highly articulate and intelligent young man; a man in his late twenties who was athletic and strong; a man capable of moods which would switch from quiet, if eccentric, charm to a wild aggression that bordered upon violence. So he never let James out of his sight, and the people of Redcoat's Green became accustomed to meeting James out for a walk wearing his yellow garb and carrying a green parasol over his head, with the attendant shadowing him five paces behind. It did not take the sharp country mind long to work out that the man was not a 'servant' as Sarah Lucas described him – but a guard. According to Dr Tuke the man remained with the family for two years. He was dismissed, not because he couldn't cope, but because Sarah Lucas could not bear to see her son restrained in such a fashion. It was an unwise move in which Sarah had allowed the emotions of a doting mother to overrule sane medical advice. By persuading her to get rid of his minder James had removed the final barrier to the freedom he wanted. With the man gone he had complete dominance over his mother; he was the Master of the House and therefore free to indulge in whatever idiosyncracies he fancied.

By the middle of the 1840s, apart from the servants, mother and son were the only regular occupants of Elmwood. James' youngest sister Emma had married Edward Walker, a wealthy London lawyer, and had moved back to the capital where she was raising her own family at a large house in Oxford Terrace, which is now part of Sussex Gardens. Brother George had qualified as a barrister but, having his own personal fortune, never practised. He never married either, but lived with an elderly spinster aunt, Harriet Lucas, at 226 Marylebone Road. In the Victorian census returns he is described as 'a landed proprietor' with a resident house staff of a footman, housekeeper and three housemaids. However, he made regular visits to Hertfordshire to help his mother with the administration of the estate. For most of the time, though, she was alone with James.

George's visits were much-resented by James, who believed he alone should control affairs at Elmwood but was quite incapable of doing so because of his steadfast refusal to conform with the basic laws of the country. As he dressed to flout convention so, too, did he select a line in politics and religion which conveniently gave him the excuse to defy authority. He had to delve back nearly 200 years into English history to find the line that suited him, but find it he did. James wasn't a Roman Catholic – his family were Irish Protestants – but he selected as his hero James II, the Stuart king who – in 1688 – was forced to flee the country after failing to impose his ardent catholicism on a reluctant Protestant nation. That, so far as James Lucas was concerned, was when the rot had set in. The nation had forced the rightful King of England into exile and allowed the country to be taken over by a crowd of foreigners. First the Dutchman William III and later that bunch of distant German cousins from Hanover, the first of whom – George I – couldn't even speak English when he plonked his arse upon our throne in 1714!

While a convert to the Jacobite cause, James remained a staunch Tory to the end of his days. In 1830 – the year his father died – there had been that General Election which had brought to an end the social scandal of parliament itself, where diehard Tories had been concerned more with protecting the wealth and privileges of the aristocracy than with relieving the appalling plight of the poor. After 50 years in opposition the Whigs came to power and, under Lord John Russell, set about reforming parliament to give the middle-classes better representation. This they did by removing the so-called 'rotten boroughs' which had given totally unfair Tory representation in the Commons. Notable was one such borough in Cornwall where two local land-owners each had a parliamentary seat to which they were both regularly returned by one voter! These 'rotten' seats were taken and distributed among the new industrial towns of the Midlands and North where the industrialists had had no representative in Parliament. However, the Tories still held sway in the House of Lords, which threw out the Bill proposing these reforms. In a long and traumatic year of rioting and arson the homes of many Tory politicians were attacked, looted and burnt, and Britain came close to civil war.

It was the elderly King William IV who saved the day by agreeing to create sufficient new Whig peers to overcome the Tories in the Lords. That threat was sufficient to bring the Upper House to heel and in June 1832 The Great Reform Bill became law and parliamentary government in Britain was transformed. King William had succeeded his brother George IV – the former high-living Prince Regent. He had never expected to become king but in the seven years that he reigned he helped to stabilise the country and raised the prestige of the British Monarchy from the abyss of waste and scandal into which it had been lowered by his late and little-lamented brother. James Lucas didn't see it that way, of course. To him, King William's connivance with the Whigs to subdue the Tories was one more act of treachery by the hated House of Hanover. Consequently, when King William died in 1837 and was succeeded by his young and beautiful niece Victoria, it was more than Lucas could take and he launched his own personal campaign against the youthful Queen. From the day of her accession until the day he died Lucas refused to sign any documents that bore stamps or any other writing or seals that in any way acknowledged the authority of Her Majesty the Queen, one good reason why brother George had to assume responsibility of the Elmwood estate.

James refused to change his beliefs and, just as he refused to acknowledge the House of Hanover, so too did he declare himself a Jacobite until the end of his days. Was it by coincidence or careful planning that the man James Lucas chose as his hero king bore the same name as himself and was, like Lucas, a social outcast? Coincidence or careful planning that the House of Hanover, which he chose to condemn, had four successive kings bearing the name of George – the talented and much-envied younger brother of whom the hermit was later to have such an obsessive fear?

For the present James was able to do as he liked. Under his medical attendant he had been obliged to confine his horsemanship to the parkland of the Elmwood estate but there came a time when he decided to venture further afield and hunt with the local hare hounds. He joined Mr Jepps' Harriers and astonished supporters and huntsmen alike by turning out in the same exotic clothes that he wore while riding at home. A remarkable sight, therefore, as he joined in the chase tied to his horse by several yards of cord, waist-length hair and yellow coat-tails flying behind him in the wind! 'People stare at us very much,' he remarked to a fellow huntsman while hacking home one evening. 'Well,' replied his colleague, 'Either you or I must look very strange. I leave you to say which it is.' Neither did James always finish riding at dusk. More than once did local topers, weaving their way home from the Wymondley beerhouses, suffer a premature release of the evening's ale after encountering the sudden appearance of a half-naked horseman galloping towards them and singing at the top of his voice.

It was while riding his mare Junie past the lych-gate of St Ippolyt's Church just before Matins one Sunday that James saw and fell in love with Miss Margaret Isabella Amos. Isabella, as she was known, was the daughter of Andrew Amos – a landowner and former judge in India – who lived about two miles from Redcoat's Green on the old London Road leading out of Hitchin. The family house, St Ibb's, to this day sits rather majestically in parklike grounds at the foot of the hill from St Ippolyt's Church, though it has now been sold and divided up into several units. It was the habit of the Amos family either to walk or take their carriage up through the park to church each Sunday morning, and when James discovered this he began to cause the family considerable annoyance and embarrassment by lying-in-wait at the top of the hill with his pony to 'greet' the delightful Miss Isabella. This he did by mounting Junie and getting her to prance and curvet in the young lady's honour, following the family almost to the church door and clapping his hands in delight. The family tried to ignore him but the matter soon got beyond a joke. James began to pester Isabella incessantly. First, he caught a couple of doves from the dove-cote that graced the wall of Elmwood House, placed them in a cage and had them delivered to St Ibb's. When they were returned, he took to prowling round the Amos's estate and persecuting the besieged girl by shouting alternate messages of love and abuse at her bedroom window. Daniel Hack Tuke, who records the story, says 'He persecuted her sadly, haunting the grounds at night and prowling round the house.' How long this was allowed to go on is not known, but descendents of the Amos family, who still own the major part of the St Ibb's estate, recall their ancestor's belief that it was Isabella's rejection of Lucas that caused him to become a recluse.

Indeed, this has been the popular theory for more than a hundred years. In a chapter on the hermit in his book *Hitchin Worthies*, published in 1932, the local historian Reginald Hine says that when Isabella married The Reverend Lewis Hensley, Vicar of Hitchin, Lucas transferred his affections to his mother and (quoting a sentence from Tuke's report) 'vowed that the hour of her death should be that of *his* death too'. However, Mr Hine – like most people – seems to have been so attracted by this story of unrequited love that he failed to notice one strange discrepancy in the dates for this period, because by the time Isabella married Lewis Hensley in 1857, Lucas's mother had already been dead for eight years! It was while seeking a reason for this anomaly that a new and far more fascinating disclosure came to light. Research among Hertfordshire newspapers preserved at the British Library's Newspaper Library at Colindale, North London, produced a sequence of facts and dates that would seem to establish beyond doubt that – at the age of 35 –

James Lucas had declared his love for a girl who could not have been more than 12 years old at the time and was probably younger than that!

Canon Lewis Hensley (1824–1905), who achieved recognition as the author of the hymn 'They Kingdom Come O God', first came to Hitchin when he was appointed Vicar of St Ippolyt's in 1856. A few months after his arrival he became Vicar of Hitchin itself and his obituary records that he married Margaret Isabella Amos the following year. During the next two years the young couple had a daughter and a son and then, in 1860, tragedy struck. While the family was at St Leonard's-on-Sea in September of that year, Isabella gave birth to their third child, a daughter. Within a fortnight Isabella, her newborn daughter and two-year-old son Arthur had died from an unknown illness. The young vicar's terrible bereavement was, of course, widely reported at the time, but the significant fact to emerge from these reports was that Isabella was only 23 when she died. As there is irrefutable evidence that the hermit never left Elmwood House and its grounds after the death of his mother in 1849 his persecution of Isabella Amos must have occurred before that date – and if Isabella was only 23 when she died in 1860 then, prior to 1849, she was but a child.

The probability that paedophilia was another of James Lucas's mental afflictions gains strength from numerous independent reports of his preference for the company of immature girls during his years as a hermit. Of all the personal reminiscences that have been passed down through Hertfordshire families, none is more frequent than those of grandmothers and great-grandmothers who could remember, as children, being taken to see Hermit Lucas. They all had a similar story to tell, of being offered sweets or bright silver coins – threepenny joeys, fourpenny groats and sixpences – if they would put a hand through the bars of his cell to allow him to kiss it. Mrs Annie Gurney of Hitchin vividly remembered the print of Lucas's sooty kiss on the back of her hand, having refused a fortune of five shillings for leave to kiss her lips. There is even confirmation from the hermit himself who, according to the *Hertfordshire Express*, once told a visitor: 'I never took a wife, but if ever I did I should like to have a girl, from eight to nine years of age, so that I could bring her up after my own mind, and then I could love her all my life time.'

To understand Lucas's predilection for little girls it is necessary at this point in his story to understand his illness. In 1874 Dr Tuke formed the opinion that the hermit's case was 'Primarily one of Moral Insanity – a madness of action rather than of language – a state of degraded feeling rather than intellectual capacity.' An emotional insanity, in fact, for which Tuke adopted the word Monomania. At this time Tuke and his colleagues had still not reached the idea that a person can be logical and at the same time insane. By modern psychiatric definition James Lucas was a paranoid schizophrenic – suffering from that more severe form of mental illness in which the patient loses touch with reality. Lucas, like all schizophrenics, was capable of quite rational behaviour but in certain directions his behaviour was governed by delusional ideas, ideas which to the sane seem completely nonsensical, but to the schizophrenic are completely and utterly real.

The fact that there was a history of eccentricity and possible insanity in this branch of the Lucas family meant that James was born with a psychopathic personality. Although it is difficult to establish precisely when the illness of paranoid schizophrenia developed, the harsh treatment for ringworm which James endured as a small boy very likely contributed to the disturbance of his emotional development; the child-like quirks of ignoring unpleasant things by shutting his eyes, of hiding in his room and refusing to return crockery were all signs of his reluctance to leave the period of his life before the ringworm and before the birth of his younger brother – when he was the centre of his parents' and his sisters' love and attention and when he was most happy. Much of that happiness stemmed from Sarah Lucas's excessive mother-love for the boy who had replaced her first-born son, lost in infancy. James was able to exploit his mother's love right through manhood in order to get his own way. Because of this, Sarah became the only sexual female that mattered to him. No other adult female would be allowed to interfere with that and so – as an outlet for his sexual feelings – he chose harmless, immature girls. But, as with any relationship between a little boy and a little girl, those feelings probably never went beyond the desire for a kiss.

That said, Lucas's obsession with Isabel Amos would have been a frightening experience for the child, particularly when he resorted to prowling round the grounds of St Ibb's during the night. His rejection by the Amos family would, at the same time, have had a fairly devastating effect on the sick mind of a man who was used to getting his own way in almost everything and although that rejection was not the main reason that he became a hermit, it would have been a contributory factor. The real cause of his seclusion was about to take place.

It is said that the illness of a paranoid schizophrenic becomes fully apparent during the third and fourth decades of the person's life. So it was with James. At the age of 35 he became aware that he was about to lose his most treasured possession. His mother was dying. George and Emma, unaware of the complexities of their brother's illness, had always been sceptical about James' declared love for their mother, arguing that though loud in his protestations of affection, he never showed it by doing a single thing she wished. To him, though, that love was real and, in his own strange way, he sought to prevent her death by any means possible. So he told his mother that when she died he would kill himself. Doctor Tuke reports that Sarah was frequently alarmed by these threats as James tried to force his mother to stay alive with the thought that by her own death she would also – indirectly – be killing her beloved son. At the time Sarah was a frail woman of 72 and it's not difficult to comprehend the mental torment she must have suffered during the last weeks of her life. Somewhat harder to imagine are the bizarre events which followed.

When Sarah died on 24 October 1849 only three of her five children survived her. The oldest daughter Anna, Countess de Taaffe, had died three years earlier at the age of 37 and is buried with her husband in the Lucas family vault at Hackney. Of the second daughter Harriet, nothing was heard after her marriage into the Polish aristocracy. Under their grandfather's will the three surviving children – James, Emma and George – stood to inherit the Elmwood estate on Sarah's death. Under normal circumstances James, as the elder brother, would have been appointed executor but as circumstances were not normal it was hardly surprising that, when the will was read, the younger brother George, a lawyer, was named as executor. What poor George could not have known at the time was that it would be thirty years before the estate was finally settled and he and his sister received the share to which they were entitled.

However, during the weeks immediately after his mother's death, the will was the least of George's worries – he had first to sort out the matter of getting the poor woman buried. The macabre events in Elmwood House during the winter of 1849 have left in their wake such a host of stories that it is impossible to extract an entirely accurate account of what happened. What *is* known is that when the Hitchin undertaker Mr Isaac Newton called to collect the deceased lady to convey her to London for burial in the Hackney cemetery, James Lucas refused to let the undertaker take her. That was on 24 October 1849. Mr Newton eventually got his hands on the coffin 13 weeks later.

What happened between those dates has been a source of speculation ever since. Most extraordinary of the stories told was that supplied by an anonymous man, signing himself 'T', to the *Hertfordshire Express* shortly after the hermit's death. He declared that Lucas made use of the medical knowledge he acquired while a youth from Dr Hicks of Whitwell and embalmed his mother's body himself, placing her in a glass coffin in the drawing room of Elmwood House. The *Hertfordshire Mercury* reported that Lucas 'had her corpse strongly encased and for 13 weeks he sat at the head of it – night and day – absorbed in inconsolable grief.' The same newspaper records that when Sarah had been dead nearly a month, Lucas employed a well-known London photographer to take a photograph of the corpse. If such a photograph were taken it has never been found. In 1849 there were very few professional photographers in London and they were still working with the rather limiting daguerrotype process which involved making individual portraits on silver-covered copper plates which could not be reproduced. The photographers worked principally in brightly-lit studios, and it seems doubtful that a portrait of a corpse in an unlit room on a dull November day could have been successfully taken.

These stories also assume that when Sarah Lucas died she was alone in the house with her son. In fact, servants were still employed and it is unlikely that George and Emma were not told of their mother's last illness and that they would not have been at her bedside during her last hours. A more rational account of events would be that – having engaged Isaac Newton to perform the last offices for their mother and seen her safely coffined in the drawing room to await her last journey to London – George and Emma made the mistake of returning to their London homes and leaving James alone with her. As a result, when Mr Newton returned with the horse-drawn hearse to collect the coffin he found Elmwood House bolted and barred. Daniel Hack Tuke says in his report that Lucas 'kept her body in the house from 24 October 1849 to the January of 1850'.

Each day he would say she might be buried tomorrow. This suggests that Newton made repeated discreet calls at the house for some time before the rest of the family had resolved what action to take. For them it was a distressing, not to say highly embarrassing predicament. So well had James secured the house that it was impossible to get in without forcing an entry, and to force an entry to grab the coffin would be highly undignified and likely to attract attention. Thus, for 13 weeks – through his 36th birthday and the Christmas of 1849 – James was allowed to sit in stubborn grief beside the corpse of his mother, determined that even in death she should not be allowed to leave him. He wanted her still, preserved in the house among the furniture and family belongings where she and they could remind him of happier days. They would continue to 'live' together as before, and nobody would be allowed to part them. But parted they were – on 20 January 1850 when Inspector Charles Goode and P.C. Wilson of Stevenage broke down the front door of Elmwood House. Accompanied by George Lucas, The Reverend Henry Wiles (then Vicar of Hitchin) and the patient undertaker Mr Newton, Inspector Goode read an order claiming the body of Sarah Lucas under Public Health regulations and 'the law of sepulchre'. Lucas offered no resistance. The long-suffering and long-dead lady was finally conveyed to London to be laid in the family vault with her husband Philip and the children who had died before her.

The unavoidably brutal removal of his mother from a genuinely grieving son was the catalyst that released the full paranoia that turned James Lucas into a hermit. His inability to resolve his grief and the shock of the enforced parting from his mother by Authority shattered him. Any confidence he had was gone and – like hermits before and since – he withdrew from society into Elmwood House and stayed there until that day in April 1874 when once again the policemen of Stevenage would be called to break down the door. Above all he now had a paranoid fear of the younger brother who had engineered the cruel removal of his beloved mother. It was a fear that remained with him for the rest of his life, causing him days of mental anguish and bringing him on occasions close to starvation. For he firmly believed that, having seized his mother, George Lucas would return to seize Elmwood and that George would one day kill him.

Inside the house he repaired and strengthened the barricades he had first put up during the period that he'd been under siege with his mother's corpse. He collected together the small number of weapons that were kept at Elmwood – a pistol, a shotgun, swords and foils – and put them together in one room. He carefully loaded each firearm and then sat to wait for the attack. The life of James Lucas, The Mad Hermit of Hertfordshire, had begun.

# 5

# THE LUNACY COMMISSIONERS, TRAMPS AND ATTEMPTED MURDER
(1851–1860)

Lucas went into seclusion a man of immense wealth, owning property and company shares that in these days would have made him a millionaire. His relatives had taken no account of his state of mind when they considered how their property should be divided, and when they died James received his fair share of their possessions. In all he benefited from three wills. His grandfather had left him a share of the Elmwood estate, his father had set up a trust fund under which James received the income from a large number of shares in the Imperial Gas Company and the London and North Western Railway Company, and his mother had left him much of the land she had owned in Cheshire and Bedfordshire. However, the hermit's steadfast refusal to put his signature to any paper remotely connected with that Hanoverian usurper Queen Victoria meant that neither the family, nor their bankers and lawyers, could do anything to tidy up what was fast becoming a financial and legal mess. Tenants paid him money but received no receipts. Some gave up paying after a while and for years lived in his property rent-free. Share dividends arrived by post at Elmwood but were ignored. Cheques, banknotes and dividend warrants lay everywhere, littering the house. The Corporation of Liverpool had endless problems trying to acquire compulsorily land in Birkenhead which Lucas had inherited from his mother and which was needed for a development project. The hermit was totally uninterested, ignoring all letters written to him; and when the land was eventually obtained under a court order for compulsory purchase – and a cheque for thousands of pounds was sent to him – he threw it away. The Corporation eventually paid the money into the Bank of England where it lay unclaimed for 25 years.

For a short period after his mother's death James allowed one servant, William Neale, to remain in the house, but as conditions inside began to deteriorate the man asked to leave, unable to cope with the bizarre behaviour of his master. There is no doubt that the hermit continued to experience a fierce grief at the loss of Sarah for years after her death. Daniel Hack Tuke reported that a neighbouring farmer had assured him that Lucas's distress was genuine and that he would weep bitterly whenever he mentioned her name. As in the case of Señora Romero and her daughter in New York in the following century, Lucas's 'unresolved grief reaction' was to try to keep everything at Elmwood as it was before his mother's death. In the bedroom where Sarah died, the bed was neatly re-made and her letters, jewellery and money were left untouched. Her favourite books of religious poetry remained in place on the bedside table, and down in the Elmwood cellars the large stock of wine was – he decided – never to be drunk. Her family coach, locked away in the coach-house, was never driven again. Even the stack nearby, built from hay cut in the Elmwood meadows during her last summer was – he ordered – never to be used.

Throughout the spring of 1850 James was seen only occasionally by his neighbours when he ventured nervously out of the house into the yard – a shambling figure dressed in a horse-rug who would scuttle back inside at the first sound of approaching footsteps. The neighbours, not unnaturally, became concerned for his welfare and gradually one or two tried to gain his confidence. The first to achieve this were his tenant, farmer Jacob Chapman, and another neighbouring farmer, Thomas Hailey. Mr Hailey supplied the hermit with milk and eggs, and persuaded James to let him take the horses – including the beloved 'Junie' – over to his farm to look after them. As this trust increased Hailey and Chapman were able to discern something of the lifestyle James had adopted inside Elmwood. Having accepted that he needed to retain some contact with the world outside and yet still protect himself from the feared attack by his brother, he had secured the rest of the house and moved into the kitchen area at the rear of the building. The windows of this room were already fitted with stout iron bars, through which he could converse with people in complete safety. So the kitchen became, in effect, a hermit's cell – stripped of most of its furniture save for a couple of chairs and a cheap table. Lucas once told a friend: 'I haven't slept in a bed for 40 years. My father used to tell me a hard bed was good for my health.' So there was no bed, the occupant preferring to sleep on the pile of cinders which accumulated from the fire he kept burning day and night; cinders which – as in his youth – he refused to have taken out of the room. He wore only the horse-rug, fastened loosely around his body with a skewer or belt. Cinders clung to it like burrs. He had nothing on his feet and, though begrimed with soot and ash which abounded in the squalid room, he never washed. He never brushed, combed, nor cut his hair and his finger and toenails grew to resemble talons. Gradually his entire body – covered by an ever-thickening film of grease and grime– turned grey and then almost black. Only his bright eyes could be clearly discerned beneath the long, matted hair and the wild, straggling beard that hid much of his face. The transformation did not take many months to complete – a hermit of old, a wild biblical figure sitting amid the trappings and fast-decaying elegance of an upper-class Victorian household.

In religious matters James was as unconventional as in everything else. He had declared himself to be a Tractarian, and in 1850 Tractarians were far from popular. Their philosophy stemmed from the Oxford Movement, a group of theologians led by J H (later Cardinal) Newman who had set about trying to prove that the doctrines of the Church of England and the Church of Rome were similar and therefore that every Papal doctrine should also be held by the Anglicans. They took their name from the Tracts they published and preached putting forward their arguments. Their insidious campaign began to anger the staunchly Protestant English, and that anger turned to alarm when, in 1845, most of the group seceded to the Roman Church. The English fears of a Vatican takeover bid reached fever pitch in September 1850 when Pope Pius IX issued a papal bull (or decree) setting up a hierarchy of bishops in England who were to derive their titles from new English sees created by the Pope. The Whig government under Lord John Russell was with the people in their vehement opposition to what had become known as 'the papal aggression' and moved swiftly to bring in a bill to prevent the bishops from assuming titles from United Kingdom territories. Some of the half-million Catholics in Britain experienced a pretty rough time at the hands of Protestant zealots, and the hermit was among them. He wasn't a member of the Roman Church, of course, but his pronouncements about the Catholics and his hero James II, coupled with his Irish background meant, so far as the stolid working-class Protestants of agricultural Hertfordshire were concerned, that he was a Papist.

The attack on Elmwood House came in the dead of night. Nobody ever found out how many were involved in the sortie but there were sufficient, armed with small rocks and stones, to break just about every window in the building, and to shatter many tiles on the roof. Lucas, not surprisingly, was terrified. He seized his firearms – shotgun and pistol – and fired several shots blindly through the shattered windows. No-one appears to have been hit but it was sufficient to make the gang flee. That was the account given by George Lucas. James' version was different. The attack was not a demonstration of anti-Catholic feeling; it had been engineered by George, who had paid a group of thugs to attack the house, break in and kill him. The hermit's paranoid fear of being murdered by his brother had been, to him, more than justified.

So it was that in the Spring of 1851, while hundreds of navvies were busy in Hyde Park constructing The Crystal Palace for Prince Albert's Great Exhibition, building work of a different kind was proceeding apace out at Redcoat's Green as Elmwood House began to assume the appearance for which it, too, was to become famous. On Lucas's instructions estate tenants arrived bearing dozens of sections of rough-hewn timber which were bolted six at a time across each of the main windows, each section held firmly in place by strong iron rivets that passed right through the wall of the house to be fixed to metal plates on the inside. The broken glass in the windows was not replaced. It would be easier, the hermit said, to 'peg away' at the attackers with his guns if there were no glass in the windows. The operation was completed and the house a fortress before George Lucas could do anything about it, and when he saw it – that was the moment when he decided to take positive lawful action to get his brother removed.

The sister Emma had already declared – after the humiliating scandal of her mother's burial – that she would have nothing more to do with James and, indeed, she never saw him again. So it was left to her husband Edward Walker and her brother George to put their legal minds together; they decided that the only way they could overcome the immense legal problem of the inheritances was to have James officially certified a lunatic and then obtain a High Court order for his affairs to be placed in the hands of trustees. The Commissioners of Lunacy – who had to consider the application – had been in existence only six years. Under the Lunacy Act of 1845 they had been invested with considerable powers to try to bring about a uniform and humane procedure for the treatment of patients in lunatic asylums. Those powers were wide-ranging and gave them, among other things, the authority to examine and detain what were described as 'neglected lunatics'. From its formation until 1885 the Commission worked under the chairmanship of the 7th Earl of Shaftesbury and it was he who – during that glorious hot Summer of 1851 – had to help decide the fate of James Lucas. A record of the Commission's deliberations is preserved at the Public Record Office at Kew but it consists only of the secretary's notes made in the Minute Book of the Commissioners of Lunacy

(Vol. Five) for that year. There are tantalising references to written evidence and interviews with witnesses, no records of which appear to have been preserved. However, there is sufficient in the Secretary's notes to follow the line the inquiry took:

'17 July 1851. Neglected Lunatic – Lucas. A gentleman of property at Titmore Green near Stevenage. Secretary reported to the Board the information he had received from Mr Timothy Maber relative to the unprotected and pitiable condition of an insane gentleman named Lucas residing in an old mansion at Titmore Green near Stevenage. Read correspondence from Mr J Povate and Mr Chapman, both of Titmore Green and Mr G Lucas of 216 Edgeware Road. Mr Geo Lucas was requested to attend the next Board.

'24 July 1851. Mr Geo Lucas attended, accompanied by his solicitor Mr Walker of the firm of Lake and Walker of Lincolns Inn Fields, the latter of whom did not express any desire to be present during the examination. Mr G Lucas stated: "My brother James and myself lived with our mother who died in October 1849, in the family house where my brother now resides called Elm Wood, near Stevenage. Upon my mother's death a respectable man was left with him who did not remain long. Brother lives chiefly on bread and milk, for which and all other necessaries I pay. No medical man has seen him of late. His income is about a thousand a year, derived chiefly from funded property received by trustees of the father's will. He never goes beyond the yard of the house, wears little, if any, ragged clothing. Understands what is said to him. Is the older brother – has some sisters who never see him. Believe that he keeps loaded firearms and have been told that he threatens to take lives with them.'

After hearing the evidence from George, Lord Shaftesbury and the Board adjourned the hearing until other witnesses could be called, and on 14 August four men travelled up from Hertfordshire to London to be interviewed – three policemen and Thomas Hailey the farmer and friend of the hermit. A fifth man, the Chief Constable of Hertfordshire Captain Archibald Robertson, submitted written evidence. After questioning the three policemen – Inspector Charles Goode of Ware (who had formerly been at Stevenage), Inspector Samuel Evans and Police Constable Wilson (who were then stationed at Stevenage) the Commission interviewed Mr Hailey. With infuriating brevity the Minute Book records only that 'Mr Hailey, farmer, of Great Wymondley, also attended and was examined relative to Mr Lucas's case (see notes of his examination)'. Whatever that evidence it was not sufficient to convince the Commission that Lucas was a lunatic. No doubt all the witnesses pointed out that – eccentricities and dirty way of life apart – the hermit was basically an articulate and intelligent man with whom it was quite possible to carry on a normal coversation. So – unaware of the complexities of James' mental illness – the Commission decided to make no order for a medical examination. Instead, as the Minute Book records: 'Mr Hailey, at the suggestion of the Board, promised to use his influence with Mr Lucas for the purpose of inducing him to change his habit of life and a letter was directed to Captain Robertson requesting him to watch the case and report at a future period.'

The prospect of an investigation into his state of mind prompted Lucas to take two – for him – highly unusual steps. He asked Thomas Hailey to engage a solicitor to represent him before the Board and placed an order with the Hitchin tailor George Groom for a new suit of clothes. Neither lawyer nor suit were needed. The lawyer, Mr Marshall Turner of Lincolns Inn Fields, wrote to the Commissioners asking what they intended to do about his client, and his letter was considered at their meeting on 21 August. Mr Turner was told by return of post 'that the result of the inquiry was to satisfy the Commissioners that Mr Lucas's case at present was not one in which they could with propriety interfere.' The day after this news had been relayed to James Mr Groom sent a messenger to Elmwood House bearing a parcel that contained the suit that had been ordered. The parcel was accepted – but never unpacked.

Although the attempt to have him certified insane had failed, the hermit gained little peace of mind from his victory. It served only to remind him that he must be ever on his guard. First, George had come and forcefully seized the body of his mother, then he'd sent hooligans to stone Elmwood and try to kill him. Having failed with that attempt he'd tried to get him put away in a lunatic asylum by getting his neighbours to testify against him. What would he attempt next? Lucas's paranoid fear of his brother totally dominated his mind and his life inside the barricaded mansion became one of terror and utter loneliness. At night, the slightest sound outside had him prowling from room to room armed with shotgun or pistol and peering anxiously through the timber baulks across the windows. Weeks went by but, of course, no attack came. Then, one day, Lucas decided that George would be too clever to try the same trick twice. He would have to find another way of killing him. But how? Of course! The only thing that the hermit allowed into the house was his modest supply of food and drink. That's how George would get at him next time – by putting poison in his food and drink!

For more than a year George had been paying all the small bills which his brother had been running up; Farmer Hailey for the milk and eggs, a local fishmonger for the occasional mackerel or herring, a baker for the bread he delivered. During that time Mr Hailey had been in the habit of sending a can of milk across each morning – a job usually entrusted to a group of village boys who were told to leave the full can on the window ledge of the hermit's kitchen cell. It was they who convinced James that his latest theory about his brother was correct, for when he drank the milk one day it tasted vile. To quote the pub and field talk of the day – 'one of them young buggers had pissed in it.' True or false, the incident with the adulterated milk prompted the hermit to take further protective action. He ordered a new milk can, fitted with a padlock, and the only people with keys were himself and his trusted friend Thomas Hailey. To foil an attempt to poison his bread supply James took to placing orders with several bakers who would arrive sometimes together with their trade carts. Each week they would take part patiently in the same strange ritual – each man standing before the window with his basket of loaves from which, after much hesitation and deliberation, the hermit would select one. Even then his confidence would go and he'd choose a second from another basket. Sometimes he would select as many as six and – when the bakers had departed – would sit there agonising over which of the six was safe to eat. It was a fear which assumed terrifying proportions. Choosing the loaf became like a game of Russian Roulette. He would sit there for hours, picking one up, putting it down, picking up another. Sometimes the selection process went on through the night until the pangs of hunger forced him to take a cautious bite. When he found it had no ill effect he would tear at it ravenously until it had been devoured. The other loaves were then thrown away onto the pile of cinders accumulating in the room. Lucas's fear of poisoned bread remained with him throughout his life. The bakers didn't mind – any customer prepared to buy six loaves in order to eat one was well worth cultivating.

Working through Thomas Hailey, George Lucas continued to settle the modest bills his brother ran up until the middle of the 1850s but there came a time when somebody had to be delegated to try to persuade James to give way over his stubborn refusal to touch legal or financial documents. The task fell to the hermit's namesake, a quietly-spoken and humorous member of the local Quaker Lucas family, Francis Lucas. A lawyer by training, he had recently joined the Hitchin bank of Sharples, Tuke, Lucas & Seebohm, who had handled the Elmwood Lucas's finances for some years. After discussions with George, Francis rode over to Redcoat's Green from Hitchin and spent most of one morning talking to the hermit through the bars of his cell window. His gentle manner won him the hermit's confidence as he explained that – while respecting his views – James' refusal to conform to normal banking procedures was causing a good deal of hardship and inconvenience to many innocent people. The bank had a solution which could be satisfactory to both parties. If James would give the bank power of attorney to handle his affairs by signing the agreement Francis had brought, then James need never have to sign a document or receipt bearing the Queen's image again. James looked over the agreement which, at this stage, bore no stamps, Royal coat-of-arms or anything else associated with Queen Victoria, and signed it. Francis Lucas was allowed into the house to collect all the paper money, dividend warrants and cheques that he could find. There was more than a thousand pounds in all. Back at the bank a stamp was belatedly added to the signed agreement and the filthy, stained warrants and cheques were sent to Lombard Street to be cashed.

From then on the bank was able to keep the hermit's financial affairs in some order. It handled the income he received from his late father's trust fund and began amassing the considerable fortune, most of which he was never to use. As his bank balance grew, he was content to live on less than £200 a year. The bank also discovered that there was a contradiction in Lucas's Anti-Victoria Campaign. For some reason never explained he did not object to handling coins bearing the Queen's image, so each week a clerk was sent over to Elmwood bearing two small bags of coins – one of copper, the other of small silver – for James to pay tradesmen and suchlike. He was also prepared to sign blank cheques, though he must have known they would be stamped later on. Between them, farmers, tradesmen and bankers had managed to bring some sort of order and routine to the administrative affairs of their most eccentric customer. To make life easier for everyone concerned, Society had bent the rules just a little to help the hermit continue his existence without breaking any of his principles. James – as throughout his entire life – was still getting his own way, and having ensured this, settled down and prepared to become a celebrity. There is only one other record of his having left the house, and that was when Thomas Hailey came round to tell him that his old mare Junie had died. Lucas asked for the horse to be buried in the garden behind Elmwood House. He ordered a new blanket and a white beaver hat 'for mourning' and attired in this strange garb attended the funeral of his horse at the bottom of the garden. The new blanket was the one he wore until his death 20 years later. Although fame did not come to the Hermit of Hertfordshire overnight, there was one section of the population through which news of him spread faster than anywhere else. In the 1850s tramps and paupers formed a very large part of the community. Hitchin – regarded as one of the county's more thriving market towns – had just over 7,000 inhabitants, of whom about a thousand were registered paupers. Most were victims of the revolution in agriculture which had taken place during the preceding 20 years. First had come the Enclosure Acts, which had placed the old open fields, the commons and wastelands under the control of the wealthy landowners, dispossessing the thousands of yeoman farmers who for centuries had cultivated their small strips of land in the traditional feudal village pattern. On top of this the swift development of agricultural machinery had caused massive redundancies on the farms. Hertfordshire, like most of the southern part of England, had had its share of rick-burning and riots as unemployed farmworkers – their families at starvation point – pressed their demands for food, work and justice. Dispossessed of their tied cottages they were forced to flee to the nearest town, putting great pressure on the community. The poor housing areas became desperately over-crowded and disease was rife. To help fend off starvation families were prepared to put children five years old to work. An investigation by a Government Inspector in 1851 revealed that in the poor area of Hitchin 'the whole of the juvenile population between the ages of five and 15 is employed in plaiting schools, plaiting straw for the manufacture of hats and bonnets.' The inspector reported seeing the children packed 30 at a time in unventilated rooms measuring only 10 feet by six, working for hours in an atmosphere he described as 'foul'. The new Hitchin Union Workhouse, built by the Guardians of the local Poor Law Charity, was capable of housing 240 paupers and was constantly full. Apart from the unemployment caused by the Agricultural Revolution the crisis was worsened by the arrival in England of thousands of Irish men and women, fleeing their country after the terrible Potato Famine of 1846–47.

During her life at Elmwood Sarah Lucas had made it her habit never to turn away a tramp or beggar who called at her house until he had been fed or given money, and when they called there after her death, the hermit not only continued the practice but launched into pauper relief on a grand scale. So grand was it that towards the end of his life he was claiming to have relieved 15–20,000 vagrants! As news of his generosity spread along the grapevine of the wandering unemployed, they began to descend on him – in their dozens first, and then in their hundreds. Lucas enjoyed giving them money – so much so that the staff at the Hitchin bank estimated that he drew out as much as £300 a year in copper and small silver to distribute to the callers. He also took to ordering a gallon of gin each week, most of which was given in tots to the tramps. However, these gestures of goodwill were not entirely philanthropic, for James had learned that the drink and the alms he doled out brought him the respect he was desperately seeking, as well as unquestioning acceptance of his bizarre views on life.

Some days the tramps literally queued up to see him. Sitting cross-legged on the floor of his cell he would receive their humble respects paid from the other side of the grill. Caps were doffed, forelocks tugged. They called him 'Sir' or 'Squire' or – best of all – 'Squire James', the nickname the nation once gave to his Roman Catholic hero King James II. This was what he had been looking for! No damned lawyers and tricksters trying to invade his privacy and steal Elmwood from him. Here was a whole section of the population that was prepared to pay obsequious homage to the Court of Squire James – and he revelled in it. Most of those he chose to patronise *were* tricksters of course – of the highest order. They had to be to survive. They spun him tales of hardship carefully woven to coincide with his own experiences and beliefs. They fawned, bowed and scraped and uttered enthusiastic agreement with every silly thing he said. Anything to ensure that a coin or two was passed through to them before they left. James Lucas wasn't that easy to gull, however, and before long each claimant for relief was being subjected to pretty exhaustive interrogation.

To help him achieve this role of Grand Inquisitor the hermit adopted a new affectation. Rummaging through the family possessions in the house one day he discovered a broken Georgian spy-glass (a small monocle with a handle to it) which he started to use to great effect to scrutinise each applicant for alms. It was a pose which helped to give him authority and also to disguise the constant fear that the next caller might be another lackey sent by brother George to do him harm. Thus, for anyone visiting the hermit – be he rich or poor – the procedure was the same. Having called his name they would hear nothing for a while; then, while their eyes were adjusting to the blackness of the kitchen cell, a quiet voice would ask anxiously 'Who is it?' The name would be given and more questions would follow. During this the visitor would gradually be able to make out the figure of Lucas crouched in the furthest and darkest corner of the cell; bright eyes shining through the long, matted hair; the blanketed limbs poised in case of trouble. Then, as his confidence increased, the hermit would move slowly forward firing a string of questions in a quiet, cultured voice that was almost plaintive in tone. He sought the most minute details. Where were they born? Where was their father born? Where was their mother born? Whether their father and mother were still living and, if dead, where buried? Was the visitor married or single? Maiden name of wife? Married long? Any children? Boy or girl? and so on and so on. Until the thirst for information had been slaked conversation on general topics was impossible.

With the vagrants each of the dozens of questions was answered dutifully. Lucas always sought from them whether they were Catholic or Protestant and if Catholic – particularly Irish Catholic – they were welcomed with open arms. The Irish immigrants were always better prepared than the Protestant paupers, bringing with them letters of reference to show the hermit. Several were found lying about in the house after his death, most written by Irish priests assuring the reader that the bearer was 'recommended as a faithful servant who is sound in The Faith.' A good Catholic who could prove his faith by reciting the Hail Mary or his church's version of the Lord's Prayer was guaranteed at least threepence and a full glass of gin; those of the Church of England got a penny and half-a-glass of gin while Nonconformists got tuppence but no gin. Not surprisingly, when word of this selective process was passed back down the never-ending line of beggars heading for Redcoat's Green, an astonishing number of swift conversions took place. Indigenous Anglicans would seek tuition from the Irish and could be found crouching in the shrubbery of the Elmwood gardens trying to rattle off a convincing version of the Hail Mary before making their approach to the cell bars. It rarely worked. Others, declaring themselves to be Catholic, would be asked to recite the Lord's Prayer but would include the last lines of the Protestant version 'For thine is the Kingdom, The Power and the Glory. For ever and ever.' – not knowing that these lines were omitted in the Catholic version. At which point up would shoot the spyglass accompanied by a triumphant shout from Lucas that 'another damned Protestant' had been exposed. After that the vagrant would be made to apologise for his lies before a halfpenny was flicked contemptuously at him through the bars.

To Lucas, the dozens of questions he asked were not wasted, for he had a remarkably retentive memory and throughout his life constantly amazed visitors of all classes by recalling facts which he had discussed with them years earlier but which they, themselves, had forgotten. So the villains and the con-men were more often than not beaten at their own game. He remembered who they were, where they came from and very often had an embarrassing knowledge of where they had been since last they visited him. A tramp doffing his cap in respect would be floored by the remark: 'I thought so! That's the haircut of Hertford Gaol!' Dicing with the nation's hungry villains was dangerous sport, though; sooner or later he was bound to meet one who would beat him at his own game – and the day he did, it nearly cost the hermit his life.

It was inevitable that, as Lucas met more and more people, so stories would begin to circulate about his great wealth; that behind the facade of the filthy cell there lay in the rest of the house riches beyond the dreams of most men. The stories grew with the telling – drawers filled with sovereigns, his mother's jewellery, gold and silver ornaments. Wealth for which the hermit had no need and which could be put to far better use elsewhere. Equally it was inevitable that someone, some day, would try to get his hands on it. The name of the man who nearly killed James Lucas was never discovered and was probably not known even by the hermit. Only that he was a young Irishman. A fellow with no work who was cheerful and polite and could produce a good reference from his priest. Lucas felt sorry for him and gave him some temporary work in the kitchen garden. That evening the hermit invited the young man into the cell for a drink. He came in still carrying the long-shafted hoe he'd been using. Lucas poured the drink – the customary gin and water – into two glasses, gave one to the Irishman and went to squat on his haunches in his traditional position in the ashes before the fire. He remembered sensing a movement behind him as the hoe was swung hard through the air but could not react in time. The metal implement smashed into the back of his head, stunning him. As he lay on the floor with blood pouring from a deep two-inch wound he was sufficiently conscious to glimpse the Irishman raising the hoe a second time; as it was brought down, Lucas managed to roll a little way to one side, bringing an arm up to protect his head. This time the hoe dug into his elbow. 'The effect of this' Lucas told a friend later 'was to cause a pain which somehow restored me to full consciousness. I rolled head-over-heels, like one sees a dog roll over, and managed to get hold of a pistol which I kept on a shelf and with this in my hand I forced my assailant out of the room. Once out he made off and was never heard of again.'

The attack occurred in 1860 and was not one of the fantasies from the dark side of the hermit's mind. His account of the attack was recorded a few weeks after it happened by a Hitchin man who called on him and saw the ugly wound on the back of Lucas's head – a wound which had not healed properly because he had refused to allow a doctor to come into the house to treat him. The only fantastic aspect of the incident was that Lucas was absolutely convinced that the man was yet another in the pay of his brother George – and he said so more than once.

The man who recorded the story signed himself simply 'C' when he told it in *The Hertfordshire Express* years later after the hermit had died. The details of that visit are interesting. They reveal that – in his later forties, and despite his self-imposed deprivations – Lucas kept himself extremely fit:

'I remember calling on Mr Lucas one very cold day in the winter of 1860, when the snow was on the ground. I was accompanied by a friend and, as soon as he saw me he cried out "Ah ＿＿. Is that you? I'm short of company today." He then admitted us and he asked me to take the only seat there was in the place, such a one that it was, an old chair with no back. My friend had to sit on the cinders. Lucas himself sat down on his haunches, with his knees up to his chin, in Indian fashion, his blanket falling off. He was so accustomed to sit in this way that he could sit down and rise without any apparent effort. He had a habit of frequently getting up and warming himself before the fire, and as we were conversing he would now and then take a gulp of milk from an old black tin saucepan, which had neither handle nor lid. We sat together all the afternoon, he supplying us with as much gin and water as we cared to have.

'An incident occurred during my stay that very much amused him. He was very fond of sparring, or of a game at single stick, or of foils, or indeed of all kinds of athletic sports and he asked me to stand up to him. He said "Show us your guard ＿＿!" I stood up and he made several feints at me, but did not succeed in drawing off my guard. At length, he called an Irishman who had been staying with him for about six weeks, and said: "Patrick, go at him and try what you can do." Pat came on, and after a while, thinking he could get at me, struck out, but he was mistaken, for stepping back I gave him a blow, which sent him sprawling among the heap of bottles which were lying in the corner, much to Mr Lucas's amusement.

'I spoke to him about the manner of life he led. I said: "You were destined for a different position in life; how is it you don't lead a respectable life and fulfil what should be your destiny?" He answered with a very strong emphasis: "I am fulfilling my destiny." I replied: "But you are not doing your duty to your country nor behaving as you should do." He said: "I behave better to the world than the world behaves to me!" at the same time turning round exhibiting a severe scalp wound at the back part of his head about two inches long. This wound he said he had then recently received from an Irishman who had been receiving his hospitality. . . . Lucas said that this attack was only part of an organised scheme to murder him by his relatives. He was a most passionate man, and on one occasion when we disagreed and I rated him on the reptile life he led, he flew at the bars of his den and not only ordered me off but afterwards sent the Superintendent of Police to warn me never to go near him again. However, some few years ago I saw him and shook hands and we became friends again.'

Mr C's recollections illustrate rather well the split personality of James Lucas. To those who accepted him for what he was and agreed with his views, he could be a charming and amusing host, but if they once challenged his way of life or dared to criticise him, then he was capable of displaying an unpleasant and violent reaction. The story confirms also that, during his first 10 years as a hermit, James made friends with some of the well-to-do as well as with vagrants. One suspects that with this wealthier section of the North Hertfordshire community it became 'the thing to do' to have spent an afternoon swigging gin-and-water in the stench and filth of Squire Lucas's cell. Though none ever admitted it by name in print, numerous prominent local men were among his regular visitors. The Quakers, particularly, took him to their hearts; James and Daniel Hack Tuke, several members of the other Lucas family, and Thomas Benwell Latchmore who, in 1865, opened photographic studios in Hitchin and made an important record of Victorian life in the district. His photographs of Elmwood House were the earliest taken although, sadly, he was unable to persuade the hermit to pose for him at the window.

From conversations with these men Lucas was able to keep abreast of life and progress in the fast-changing world beyond his cell. They brought him newspapers which publicly he dismissed as 'trash' but privately read avidly from cover to cover. From them, for instance, he would have learned about the development of Britain's railway system. Alone at night he could hear the rattle of trains and the shrill whistle of the engines that passed by on the new Great Northern Line less than a mile from his home, but throughout his life he never saw a railroad nor a train. The Great Northern had opened in 1850, a year after he went into seclusion; 12 trains a day plying between London and Peterborough, with stops at Stevenage and Hitchin. By 1857 the Midland Railway Company had opened its service between Leicester and Hitchin and their trains shared the line into London with the Great Northern, with the result that the track past Lucas's estate became one of the busiest in the country. At times it was also the most confused, with more than 3,000 delays reported every year. One regular and unofficial delay on this stretch of the nation's transport system was not caused by track congestion, however. It happened many nights during the 1850s and 1860s when the crew of the night goods train from Peterborough to London would halt the train at Wymondley bridge, give a couple of blasts on the whistle to alert the hermit and then stroll across the fields to join him for a drink and a chat. Fish for Billingsgate, flowers and vegetables for Covent Garden – all had to wait while the driver, stoker and guard left their train unmanned in order to down a couple of gins apiece with The Squire! So regular was this occurrence that the night train became known among the crews as 'The Lucas Train' and the name stuck with it until well into the 20th Century.

And yet, despite the knowledge he gained from his friends on the railway, despite the fact that part of his income was derived from his late father's shares in the North Western Railway Company, James persisted throughout his life to dismiss the new railway system as 'a delusion'. More likely he meant by this 'an error' rather than 'a false belief'. For, like many die-hard Tories of the time, he believed it was dangerous to educate the lower classes beyond the elementary stage. 'I'm against education,' he once declared. 'People are happier when they are ignorant; education leads to a man getting hanged or transported.' And as for that *other* system of transportation – the railways – well, he was simply echoing the thoughts of men like the Duke of Wellington and the poet Wordsworth who were convinced that providing this cheap method of mobility for the lower classes would seriously damage the pattern and fabric of our society. Railways, however, were here to stay and in the summer of 1861 they brought to Hertfordshire and to the hermit a distinguished visitor. On Saturday 15 June Mr Charles Dickens arrived at King's Cross station with his sister-in-law Georgina Hogarth and his daughter Mamey and purchased three first-class tickets to Stevenage.

The trio were off to spend a week at Knebworth House, the home of Dickens' close friend Sir Edward Bulwer-Lytton. What followed during that week prompted Dickens to write one of the most critical portraits he ever penned against a living person. An article forgotten now by all but the keenest students of the great man's work but which, in 1861, was to turn the Hermit of Hertfordshire into a national curiosity. An article for which James Lucas never forgave the writer.

# 6

# ENCOUNTER WITH DICKENS
(1861–1862)

Charles Dickens was no stranger to Knebworth House. Throughout the 1850s and 60s the imposing mock-medieval castle – some four miles south of the hermit's mansion – had been a regular haunt for some of the most distinguished writers and dramatists of the period. The host himself was one. Sir Edward Bulwer-Lytton was Conservative Member of Parliament for Hertfordshire from 1852 until 1856 when he was elevated to the peerage and took the title Baron Lytton of Knebworth. However, he's remembered now more for his writing than for his politicking. A prolific novelist, playwright and translator who won a considerable following from the reading public of the day. Critics may have disagreed over the literary merits of his novels, but the fact remains that in 1853 his publishers gave him a £20,000 contract for a ten-year copyright on cheap editions of his collective works. Lytton and Dickens worked together on a number of literary projects during their long friendship and were responsible for The Guild of Literature and Art, a remarkable welfare scheme designed to help impoverished writers and artists.

The two men first formulated the idea of the Guild in 1850, the plan being to establish a charitable organisation that would build and fund a small colony of homes for struggling writers and painters in the grounds of Lord Lytton's estate. There, free from most worldly worries, the beneficiaries would be able to work in peace and maybe produce an outstanding literary or artistic offering that would set them on their way. To sponsor the enterprise Dickens made use of his favourite pastime of amateur theatricals and began presenting charity performances of new or popular established plays before invited guests in the homes of the aristocracy. The company – of which Dickens was actor-manager – consisted mainly of well-known writers and artists who were also enthusiastic amateur actors and for whom the fun of taking part was more important than the money they were raising for the charity. One of the earliest performances was held in the Great Hall of Knebworth House in 1850. A year later Lytton wrote a comedy *Not So Bad As We Seem* which was performed before Queen Victoria at the Duke of Devonshire's house in London. The company also went on several short provincial tours.

Another of Dickens' friends involved in the theatrical jollities at Knebworth was the historian and biographer John Forster (1812–76) whose three-volume *Life of Dickens* remains today a major source of reference for students of Dickens. Forster, of the powerful features and booming voice, stayed with the company for ten years and earned something of a reputation as a character actor. He also had dealings with the Hermit of Hertfordshire; in 1872, as a member of the Board of Lunacy Commissioners, he had to help adjudicate on a second attempt to have Lucas certified insane.

The charity performances raised large sums of money but the idea of the writers' and artists' colony at Knebworth never fully materialised. In the House of Commons Lytton made an eloquent speech which won him more than enough support for the idea, and the House passed a Charter of Incorporation to establish the Guild – but a statutory period of seven years had to pass before it could begin to make grants to establish the colony; so it was some years before it got under way. Eventually, three houses were built on the outskirts of Stevenage on land given by Lytton and he and Dickens attended a festival to mark their completion. Unfortunately the two philanthropists had underestimated the stubborn independence of Britain's struggling writers and artists. Few showed any interest in the charitable facilities on offer and after a few years the worthy Guild of Literature and Art fizzled out and was forgotten. In 1861, at the time of Dickens' visit to the hermit, it was still a going concern, although this was not the reason for the author's trip to Knebworth. Two years earlier Dickens had founded a new periodical called *All the Year Round* and he used it to publish in serial form two of the stories that became his greatest novels – '*A Tale of Two Cities*' and '*Great Expectations*'. He also published contributions by other acknowledged authors of the day, Lytton among them, and it was to discuss Lytton's latest work '*Strange Story*' that Dickens travelled to Knebworth with Georgina and Mamey that Saturday in June. The visit is mentioned briefly in Forster's biography:

'Dickens passed a week at Knebworth, accompanied by his daughter and sister-in-law, in the summer of 1861, as soon as he had closed *Great Expectations*; and there met Mr Arthur Helps (later Sir Arthur Helps, Clerk to the Privy Council) with whom and with Lord Orford he visited the so-called "Hermit" near Stevenage, whom he described as Mr Mopes in *Tom Tiddler's Ground*. With his great brother artist he thoroughly enjoyed himself, as he invariably did. . . .' In a later biography Edgar Johnson records: 'During the middle of June with Georgy and Mamey, Dickens paid a visit to Lytton at Knebworth, and saw the houses for the Guild of Literature and Art that were now rising near Stevenage. Across the road (sic) they also looked in curiously on Mr James Lucas, the Hertfordshire Hermit, a man of means who chose to live with matted hair and unwashed body, clad only in a blanket, in the foul kitchen of his decaying mansion.'

It was a visit Dickens could hardly have resisted for – just like Miss Havisham in *Great Expectations* – here was a person who might have stepped directly from the pages of one of the maestro's novels. A character from real life who – like those in Dickens' own stories – was larger than life. In fact the hermit proved rather *too* large for Mr Dickens to handle for the acrimonious encounter ended with Lucas reaching for the well-used shotgun, although on this occasion the illustrious target stood its ground and no grape-shot was discharged. There are no independent reports of precisely what happened during the interview. We have only the author's fictionalised account and the subject's vehement but rather unconvincing denials which followed. The story, which ran to 48 pages and seven chapters, was published six months later in the Christmas edition of *All The Year Round*. What may need clarification is the reason why Dickens chose to make use of the hermit in the way he did – for even by his standards it is an uncharacteristically venomous piece of prose.

As with his novels Dickens used his new magazine as a platform for his views and ideas upon every kind of social problem affecting Victorian society; the plight of the Poor, Education, Factory Conditions, Slum Clearance, Housing and so on. In 1861 when he visited James Lucas he was in the last decade of his life. Although only 49, ill health and punishing hard work had left him older than his years and – as he entered premature old age – he became preoccupied with upholding Law and Order. He remained to the end of his life a reformer, a liberal, a radical and scoffer at institutions and conventions but – as with many old people – his anxieties could be easily aroused by the more extreme forms of anti-social behaviour. Bullies, muggers, bohemians, political extremists – even tramps and groups of swearing rowdies – all worried and angered him. Such an extremist was James Lucas. What disgusted Dickens was not just the filthy way of life the hermit had adopted, but the fact that here was a man of education and wealth who was shirking his responsibilities; shutting himself away instead of making the contributions to society normally expected from people of his class. Lucas, he thought, was a poseur, adopting the hermit lifestyle in order to achieve and enjoy notoriety. It was a hopeless confrontation that day they met. On one side of the bars crouched a paranoid schizophrenic, whose sick mind told him that everything he did was right and justified. On the other stood a literary giant, unaware that his subject was suffering from a most severe form of mental illness and seeing him only as an apparently intelligent man whose refusal to accept his responsibilities in life should serve as a warning to others.

So *Tom Tiddler's Ground* was born. In compiling the story Dickens used the services of four other contributors. This kind of format was fairly common at the time – one writer would set up a topic of social concern and others would supplement it with separate stories that provided examples and illustrations of the moralistic theme the main writer had chosen. Dickens cast himself as Mr Traveller, who descends on Mr Mopes the Hermit and proceeds to taunt and lecture him about the manner in which he is wasting his life. Mr Traveller undertakes to prove 'through the lips of every chance wayfarer' who comes in at the hermit's gate that – by outlawing himself from society, by disregarding the common laws of decency – he is a poor, weak creature. The extracts reprinted show Dickens' loathing for Lucas and his lifestyle increasing almost line-by-line. Mr Mopes, he calls him, implying that Lucas is aimless and sulky. He names Elmwood *Tom Tiddler's Ground* after a popular Victorian children's game of 'dare' in which youngsters would dash over a line and pick up imaginary pieces of gold and silver without being caught by Tom Tiddler, the one who was 'it'. Tom was the hermit, the children being the swarms of tramps to whom he tossed coins. The name Tiddler also implies that Lucas was the very smallest fish in the Pond of Life. Mild phrases, though, compared with others that follow: 'Sluggard . . . The Thing . . . It . . . A slothful, unsavoury, nasty reversal of the laws of human nature.'

Although partly fictionalised, the description by Dickens of his encounter with Lucas contains many accurate points that could have been observed only during a fairly long conversation with his subject. Phrases used by the hermit are typical of those recalled by others who met him, as are the mannerisms. His conceited attitude when first approached; the petulant way he tried to get rid of his unwanted visitor by turning his back and pretending he wasn't there; the threat with the shotgun and the anxiety about possible 'confederates' waiting outside. All are typical of Lucas's behaviour. There is also the interesting exchange about tobacco. For the first 12 years of his solitude James had been an inveterate pipe-smoker, puffing 'three-penny shag' in a broken clay pipe to such an extent that it made him ill. He complained of head pains and in the very year that Dickens visited him he had given it up saying it was affecting his nerves. From that moment on he was forever cautioning smokers that the habit could damage the body and mind. This then is how the Hermit of Hertfordshire was introduced to Victorian England by the world's most widely-read author. The extracts chosen are those written by Dickens himself.

# TOM TIDDLER'S GROUND

*by*

Charles Dickens

Published in the Christmas Edition
of
ALL THE YEAR ROUND
1861

"What *is* a Hermit?" asked the Traveller.

"What is it?" repeated the Landlord, drawing his hand across his chin.

"I'll tell you what I suppose it to be," said the Traveller. "An abominable dirty thing."

"Mr Mopes is dirty, it cannot be denied," said the Landlord.

"Intolerably conceited."

"Mr Mopes is vain of the life he leads, some do say," replied the Landlord, as another concession.

"A slothful, unsavoury, nasty reversal of the laws of human nature," said the Traveller; "and for the sake of God's working world and its wholesomeness, both moral and physical, I would put the thing on the treadmill (if I had my way) wherever I found it; whether on a pillar, or in a hole; whether on Tom Tiddler's Ground, or the Pope of Rome's ground, or a Hindoo fakeer's ground or any other ground."

"I don't know about putting Mr Mopes on the treadmill," said the Landlord, shaking his head very seriously. "That ain't a doubt but what he has got landed property."

"How far may it be to this said Tom Tiddler's Ground?" asked the Traveller.

"Put it at five mile," returned the Landlord.

Mr Traveller having finished his breakfast and paid his moderate score, walked out to the threshold of the Peal of Bells, and, thence directed by the pointing finger of his host, betook himself towards the ruined hermitage of Mr Mopes the hermit.

For Mr Mopes, by suffering everything about him to go to ruin, and by dressing himself in a blanket and skewer, and by steeping himself in soot and grease and other nastiness, has acquired great renown in all that countryside – far greater renown than he could ever have won for himself, if his career had been that of any ordinary Christian, or decent Hottentot. He had even blanketed and skewered and sooted and greased himself into the London papers. And it was curious to find, as Mr Traveller found by stopping for a new direction at this farm-house or at that cottage as he went along, with how much accuracy the morbid Mopes had counted on the weakness of his neighbours to embellish him. A mist of home-brewed marvel and romance surrounded Mopes, in which (as in all fogs) the real proportions of the real object were extravagantly heightened. He had murdered his beautiful beloved in a fit of jealousy and was doing penance; he had made a vow under the influence of grief; he had made a vow under the influence of a fatal accident; he had made a vow under the influence of religion; he had made a vow under the influence of drink; he had made a vow under the influence of disappointment; he had never made any vow but "had got led into it" by the possession of a mighty and most awful secret; he was enormously rich, he was stupendously charitable, he was profoundly learned, he saw spectres, he knew and could do all kinds of wonders. Some said he went out every night, and was met by terrified wayfarers stalking along the dark roads, others said he never went out, some knew his penance to be nearly expired, others had positive information that his seclusion was not a penance at all, and would never expire but with himself. Even, as to the easy facts of how old he was, or how long he had held verminous occupation of his blanket and skewer, no consistent information was to be got, from those who must know if they would. He was represented as being all the ages between five-and-twenty and sixty, and as having been a hermit seven years, twelve, twenty, thirty – though twenty, on the whole, appeared the favourite term.

"Well, well!" said Mr Traveller. "At any rate, let us see what a real live Hermit looks like."

So, Mr Traveller went on, and on, and on, until he came to Tom Tiddler's ground.

It was a nook in a rustic by-road, which the genius of Mopes had laid waste as completely as if he had been born an Emperor and a Conqueror. Its centre object was a dwelling house, sufficiently substantial, all the window-glass of which had been long ago abolished by the surprising genius of Mopes, and all the windows of which were barred across with rough-split logs of trees nailed over them on the outside. A rickyard, hip-high in vegetable rankness and ruin, contained outbuildings, from which the thatch had lightly fluttered away, on all the winds of all the seasons of the year, and from which the planks and beams had heavily dropped and rotted. The frosts and damps of winter, and the heats of summer, had warped what wreck remained, so that not a post or a board retained the position it was meant to hold, but everything was twisted from its purpose, like its owner, and degraded and debased. In this homestead of the sluggard, behind the ruined hedge, and sinking away among the ruined grass and the nettles, were the last perishing fragments of certain ricks: which had gradually mildewed and collapsed, until they were like mounds of rotten honeycomb, or dirty sponge. Tom Tiddler's ground could even show its ruined water; for there was a slimy pond into which a tree or two had fallen – one soppy trunk and branches lay across it then – which in its accumulation of stagnant weed, and in its black decomposition, and in all its foulness and filth, was almost comforting, regarded as the only water that could have reflected the shameful place without seeming polluted by that low office.

Mr Traveller looked all around him on Tom Tiddler's ground, and his glance at last encountered a dusky Tinker lying among the weeds and rank grass, in the shade of the dwelling-house. A rough walking-staff lay on the ground by his side, and his head rested on a small wallet. He met Mr Traveller's eye without lifting up his head, merely depressing his chin a little (for he was lying on his back) to get a better view of him.

"Good day!" said Mr Traveller.

"Same to you, if you like it," returned the Tinker.

"Don't *you* like it? It's a very fine day."

"I ain't partickler in weather," returned the Tinker, with a yawn.

Mr Traveller had walked up to where he lay, and was looking down at him. "This is a curious place," said Mr Traveller.

"Ay, I suppose so!" returned the Tinker. "Tom Tiddler's ground, they call this."

"Are you well acquainted with it?"

"Never saw it afore today," said the Tinker, with another yawn, "and don't care if I never see it again. There was a man here just now, told me what it was called. If you want to see Tom himself you must go in at that gate." He faintly indicated with his chin a little mean ruin of a gate at the side of the house.

"Have you seen Tom?"

"No, and I ain't partickler to see him. I can see a dirty man anywhere."

"He does not live in the house, then?" said Mr Traveller, casting his eyes upon the house anew.

"The man said," returned the Tinker, rather irritably – "him as was just now – 'this what you're a lying on, mate, is Tom Tiddler's ground. And if you want to see Tom,' he says, 'you must go in at that gate.' The man come out at that gate himself, and he ought to know."

"Certainly," said Mr Traveller.

"Though, perhaps," exclaimed the Tinker, so struck by the brightness of his own idea, that it had the electric effect upon him of causing him to lift up his head an inch or so, "perhaps he was a liar! He told some rum 'uns – him as was here just now did about this place of Tom's. He says – him as was here just now – 'When Tom shut up the house, mate, to go to rack, the beds was left, all made, like as if somebody was a-going to sleep in every bed. And if you was to walk through the bedrooms now, you'd see the ragged mouldy bed-clothes a heaving and a heaving like seas. And a heaving and a heaving with what?' he says. 'Why, with the rats under 'em.'"

"I wish I had seen that man," Mr Traveller remarked.

"You'd have been welcome to see him instead of me seeing him," growled the Tinker; "for he was a long-winded one."

Not without a sense of injury in the remembrance, the Tinker gloomily closed his eyes. Mr Traveller, deeming the Tinker a short-winded one, from whom no further breath of information was to be derived, betook himself to the gate.

Swung upon its rusty hinges, it admitted him into a yard in which there was nothing to be seen but an outhouse attached to the ruined building, with a barred window in it. As there were traces of many recent footsteps under this window, and as it was a low window, and unglazed, Mr Traveller made bold to peer within the bars. And there to be sure he had a real live Hermit before him, and could judge how the real dead Hermits used to look.

He was lying on a bank of soot and cinders, on the floor, in front of a rusty fireplace. There was nothing else in the dark little kitchen, or scullery, or whatever his den had been originally used as, but a table with a litter of old bottles on it. A rat made a clatter among these bottles, jumped down, and ran over the real live Hermit on his way to his hole, or the man in *his* hole would not have been so easily discernible. Tickled in the face by the rat's tail, the owner of Tom Tiddler's ground opened his eyes, saw Mr Traveller, started up, and sprang to the window.

"Humph!" thought Mr Traveller, retiring a pace or two from the bars. "A compound of Newgate, Bedlam, a Debtors' Prison in the worst time, a chimney-sweep, a mudlark, and the Noble Savage! A nice old family, the Hermit family. Hah!"

Mr Traveller thought this, as he silently confronted the sooty object in the blanket and skewer (in sober truth it wore nothing else), with the matted hair and the staring eyes. Further, Mr Traveller thought, as the eyes surveyed him with a very obvious curiosity in ascertaining the effect they produced, "Vanity, vanity, vanity! Verily, all is vanity!"

"What is your name, sir, and where do you come from?" asked Mr Mopes the Hermit – with an air of authority, but in the ordinary human speech of one who has been to school.

Mr Traveller answered the inquiries.

"Did you come here, sir, to see *me*?"

"I did. I heard of you, and I come to see you – I know you like to be seen." Mr Traveller coolly threw the last words in, as a matter of course, to forestall an affectation of resentment or objection that he saw rising beneath the grease and grime of the face. They had their effect.

"So," said the Hermit, after a momentary silence, unclasping the bars by which he had previously held, and seating himself behind them on the ledge of the window, with his bare legs and feet crouched up, "you know I like to be seen?"

Mr Traveller looked about him for something to sit on, and, observing a billet of wood in a corner, brought it near the window. Deliberately seating himself upon it, he answered, "Just so."

Each looked at the other, each appeared to take some pains to get the measure of the other.

"Then you have come to ask me why I lead this life," said the Hermit, frowning in a stormy manner. "I never tell that to any human being. I will not be asked that."

"Certainly you will not be asked that by me," said Mr Traveller, "for I have not the slightest desire to know."

"You are an uncouth man," said Mr Mopes the Hermit.

"You are another," said Mr Traveller.

The Hermit, who was plainly in the habit of overawing his visitors with the novelty of his filth and his blanket and skewer, glared at his present visitor in some discomfiture and surprise: as if he had taken aim at him with a sure gun, and his piece had missed fire.

"Why do you come here at all?" he asked, after a pause.

"Upon my life," said Mr Traveller, "I was made to ask myself that very question only a few minutes ago – by a Tinker too."

As he glanced towards the gate in saying it, the Hermit glanced in that direction likewise.

"Yes. He is lying on his back in the sunlight outside," said Mr Traveller, as if he had been asked concerning the man, "and he won't come in; for he says – and really very reasonably – 'What should I come in for? I can see a dirty man anywhere.' "

"You are an insolent person. Go away from my premises. Go!" said the Hermit, in an imperious and angry tone.

"Come, come!" returned Mr Traveller, quite undisturbed. "This is a little too much. You are not going to call yourself clean? Look at your legs. And as to these being on your premises; – they are in far too disgraceful a condition to claim any privilege of ownership, or anything else."

The Hermit bounced down from his window-ledge, and cast himself on his bed of soot and cinders.

"I am not going," said Mr Traveller, glancing after him; you won't get rid of me in that way. You had better come and talk."

"I won't talk," said the Hermit, flouncing round to get his back towards the window.

"Then I will," said Mr Traveller. "Why should you take it ill that I have no curiosity to know why you live this highly absurd and highly indecent life? When I contemplate a man in a state of disease surely there is no moral obligation on me to be anxious to know how he took it."

After a short silence, the Hermit bounced up again, and came back to the barred window.

"What? You are not gone?" he said, affecting to have supposed that he was.

"Nor going," Mr Traveller replied. "I design to pass this summer day here."

"How dare you come, sir, upon my premises –" the Hermit was returning, when his visitor interrupted him.

"Really, you know, you must *not* talk about your premises. I cannot allow such a place as this to be dignified with the name of premises."

"How dare you," said the Hermit, shaking his bars, "come in at my gate to taunt me with being in a diseased state?"

"Why, Lord bless my soul," returned the other, very composedly, "you have not the face to say that you are in a wholesome state? Do allow me again to call your attention to your legs. Scrape yourself anywhere – with anything – and then tell me you are in a wholesome state. The fact is, Mr Mopes, that you are not only a Nuisance –"

"A Nuisance?" repeated the Hermit, fiercely.

"What is a place in this obscene state of dilapidation but a Nuisance? What is a man in your obscene state of delapidation but a Nuisance? Then, as you very well know, you cannot do without an audience, and your audience is a Nuisance. You attract all the disreputable vagabonds and prowlers within ten miles around, by exhibiting yourself to them in that objectionable blanket, and by throwing copper money among them, and giving them a drink out of those very dirty jars and bottles that I see in there (their stomachs need to be strong!); and in short," said Mr Traveller, summing up in a quietly and comfortably settled manner, "you are a Nuisance, and this kennel is a Nuisance, and the audience that you cannot possibly dispense with is a Nuisance, and the Nuisance is not merely a local Nuisance, because it is a general Nuisance to know that there *can* be such a Nuisance left in civilisation so very long after its time."

"Will you go away? I have a gun in here," said the Hermit.

"Pooh!"

"I *have*!"

"Now, I put it to you. Did I say you have not? And as to going away, didn't I say I am not going away? You have made me forget where I was. I now remember that I was remarking on your conduct being a Nuisance. Moreover, it is in the last and lowest degree inconsequent foolishness and weakness."

"Weakness?" echoed the Hermit.

"Weakness," said Mr Traveller, with his former comfortably settled final air.

"I weak, you fool?" cried the Hermit, "I, who have held to my purpose, and my diet, and my only bed there, in all these years?"

"The more the years, the weaker you," returned Mr Traveller. "Though the years are not so many as folks say, and as you willingly take credit for. The crust upon your face is thick and dark, Mr Mopes but I can see enough of you through it to see you are a young man."

"Inconsequent foolishness is lunacy, I suppose?" said the Hermit.

"I suppose it is very like it," answered Mr Traveller.

"Do I converse like a lunatic?"

"One of us two must have a strong presumption against him of being one, whether or no. Either the clean and decorously clad man, or the dirty and indecorously clad man. I don't say which."

"Why, you self-sufficient bear," said the Hermit, "not a day passes and I am justified in my purpose by the conversations I hold here; not a day passes but I am shown, by everything I hear and see here, how right and strong I am in holding my purpose."

Mr Traveller lounged easily on his billet of wood, took out a pocket pipe and began to fill it. "Now, that a man," he said, appealing to the summer sky as he did so, "that a man – even behind bars, in a blanket and skewer – should tell me that he can see, from day to day, any orders or conditions of men, women and children, who can by any possibility teach that it is anything but the miserablest drivelling for a human creature to quarrel with his social nature – not to go so far as to say, to renounce his common human decency, for this is an extreme case; or who can teach him that he can in any wise separate himself from his kind and the habits of his kind, without becoming a deteriorated spectacle calculated to give the Devil (and perhaps the monkeys) pleasure – is something wonderful! I repeat," said Mr Traveller, beginning to smoke, "the unreasoning hardihood of it is something wonderful – even in a man with the dirt upon him an inch or two thick – behind bars – and in a blanket and skewer!"

The Hermit looked at him irresolutely, and retired to his soot and cinders and lay down, and got up again and came to the bars, and again looked at him irresolutely, and finally said with sharpness: "I don't like tobacco."

"I don't like dirt," rejoined Mr Traveller; "tobacco is an excellent disinfectant. We shall both be the better for my pipe. It is my intention to sit here through this summer day, until that blessed summer sun sinks low in the west, and to show you what a poor creature you are, through the lips of every chance wayfarer who may come in at your gate."

"What do you mean?" inquired the Hermit, with a furious air.

"I mean that yonder is your gate, and there are you, and here am I; I mean that I know it to be a moral impossibility that any person can stray in at that gate from any point of the compass, with any sort of experience gained at first hand, or derived from another, that can confute me and justify you."

"You are an arrogant and boastful hero," said the Hermit. "You think yourself profoundly wise."

"Bah!" returned Mr Traveller quietly smoking. "There is little wisdom in knowing that every man must be up and doing, and that all mankind are dependent on one another."

"You have companions outside," said the Hermit. "I am not to be imposed upon by your assumed confidence in the people who may enter."

"A depraved distrust," returned the visitor, compassionately raising his eyebrows, "of course belongs to your state. I can't help that."

"Do you mean to tell me you have no confederates?"

"I mean to tell you nothing but what I have told you. What I have told you is, that it is a moral impossibility that any son or daughter of Adam can stand on this ground that I put my foot on, or on any ground that mortal treads and gainsay the healthy tenure on which we hold our existence."

"Which is," sneered the Hermit, "according to you –"

"Which is," returned the other, "according to Eternal Providence, that we must arise and wash our faces and do our gregarious work and act and re-act on one another, leaving only the idiot and the palsied to sit blinking in the corner. Come!" apostrophising the gate, "Open Sesame! Show his eyes and grieve his heart! I don't care who comes, for I know what must come of it!"

With that, he faced round a little on his billet of wood towards the gate; and Mr Mopes, the Hermit, after two or three ridiculous bounces of indecision at his bed and back again, submitted to what he could not help himself against, and coiled himself on his window-ledge, holding to his bars and looking out rather anxiously.

In the five following chapters the visitors awaited by the anxious hermit come through the gate and up to the window of the cell; an artist, a Frenchman, a carpenter, a merchant's clerk and a little girl. Each has a story to tell based on personal experience and each has a moral which utterly condemns the way of life adopted by the recluse. The message to Lucas was clear; unnatural solitude leads to evil thoughts and evil ways. 'If you have any wisdom,' concludes Dickens, 'come out from that demoralising hutch of yours.'

# 7

## COPING WITH VISITORS
(1862–1868)

The print had all but dried on the Christmas number of *All the Year Round* when some mischief-maker scooted over to Elmwood House to deliver a copy through the cell window. As with other newspapers and periodicals offered to him Lucas accepted it with a great show of reluctance and disinterest, making it quite clear to the donor that he would never bother to read it. As always, once alone, he settled down and avidly devoured the contents. He must have read the essay over and over again because, by the time he was prepared to discuss it, he could quote large chunks of it from memory. To the steady stream of callers who came to discover his reaction he gave the same answer. The article was the latest attempt by brother George to humiliate and injure him. All other attempts to remove him from Elmwood having failed, George had resorted to slander. He had paid Dickens – 'and paid him well, mark you' – to make up a story from hearsay, a story that was false from beginning to end.

The hermit made great play of the large amount of fiction which Dickens and his colleagues had woven into the essay, arguing that this made the *whole* story a fiction. Dickens had written of 'a little mean ruin of a gate at the side of the house' when there had been no gate there for four or five years. There was no 'billet of wood' in the yard which Dickens could have sat upon. No artist, nor Frenchman, nor carpenter, no merchant's clerk, nor tinker had dropped in to relate their moralistic tales. And when Dickens had referred on the last page to seeing the hermit lying on his bed of ashes clearly discerned through the barred window 'by the dying glow of the sunset' – well, how could that be when his cell faced East and not West?

To those who pressed him directly on whether or not he had met the author, Lucas always answered with a firm denial – and a point in his favour here is that Dickens is known to have used a false name on occasions in order to protect his real identity. Yet, having issued that denial, the hermit could never resist adding a further comment which frequently left the questioner with the thought that the meeting had taken place but Lucas wasn't going to admit it. In March 1862, three months after the article had been published, he told William Pollard of *The Herts. Guardian*: 'A man might come here and say he was Charles Dickens, and I should take no more notice of him than if he said he was John Smith; but I am certain he never introduced himself to me as the author of *The Pickwick Papers*; for, if he had, I should have told him he had written an enormous quantity of trash.' Two months later he was telling Edward Copping of *London Society* that he could give him a solemn assurance that he had never met a man called Mr Traveller – thus carefully avoiding the question of whether he had met a man called Mr Dickens!

To Charles Holmes of *The North Herts & South Beds Journal* he 'characterised the work as a blackguardly one, prefacing his condemnation with a word that would not look well in print.'

The length of time Dickens spent with Lucas was certainly not as long as the account of their conversation suggests. There was a heated exchange of sorts but it's hard to believe that all those eloquent phrases of condemnation poured from Mr Traveller's lips at the time. They were perfected later when the author's pen was in his hand. One popular theory is that Lucas ended the interview prematurely by slamming the shutters of the cell window in Dickens' face and that the author made an attempt to obtain a second interview later in the week by turning up in disguise. This story appeared in print in Ireland about three months after *Tom Tiddler's Ground* had been published. A lady from Kircubbin, County Down, had been so fascinated by her meeting with the hermit during a visit to England that she wrote a glowing account of their encounter in *The Down Recorder*, part of which is reproduced later. Right at the end she made the revelation that Dickens 'who had offended Mr Lucas terribly' returned to the house pretending to be a Highlander. She wrote: 'Mr Lucas at once began to question him about the country, and then spoke to him in Gaelic, which he could not reply to. Mr Lucas said to him, "Sir, you are an imposter; you are no gentleman".'

A nice story which was seized on by a number of other newspapers including *The Herts. Guardian.* However, what the *Guardian* did not publish (presumably because they did not hear of it) was a sequel which appeared in the same Irish newspaper a couple of weeks later. A friend of Dickens had felt the disguise incident so unlikely that he sent the author a copy of the paper with the result that Dickens himself was obliged to write a letter denying the story. The friend sent the letter to the *Down Recorder,* who published it along with an apology.

London
27th March 1862

Dear Mr Finlay,
As you sent me your paper with that very cool account of myself in it, perhaps you want to know whether or no it is true. There is not a syllable of truth in it. I have never seen the person in question but once in my life and then I was accompanied by Lord Orford, Mr Arthur Helps, The Clerk of the Privy Council; my eldest daughter and my sister-in-law; all of whom know perfectly well that nothing of the sort passed. It is sheer invention of the wildest kind.
Faithfully, yours ever,
Charles Dickens.

Though Dickens himself confirmed the visit with that letter, James Lucas continued steadfastly to deny that any such encounter had taken place. A Hitchin man who later contributed anonymously to the hermit's obituary commented: 'Though obviously smarting keenly and feeling the cap an exact fit, he strove to convince us that he cared nothing for the article.' Noting that Lucas's copy of *All the Year Round* bore signs of handwriting on its grubby pages, the visitor slyly offered to exchange it for his own, cleaner, copy; but gullibility wasn't one of the hermit's weaknesses. 'He saw through me in a moment,' the writer admitted, 'and politely requested me to examine his eye in order to discern any appearance of verdure that might exist there! Merry at his acuteness and my discomfiture, after a glass of sherry, we wished him good-day and drove off.'

If Dickens had hoped that his vitriolic satire might help to destroy Lucas's way of life he was disappointed, for it served only to turn the man into more of a national curiosity. If there was one thing that fascinated all sections of Victorian society it was an interesting freak. For the lower classes, pathetic and sometimes fraudulent examples could be seen in the shabby sideshows of the travelling fairs; others were presented as acts in the theatres and music halls and – for the rich – the very best examples could be seen at the Egyptian Hall in Piccadilly. Singing Siamese twins, two pretty negro girls, joined at the back and squeezed into one big dress were billed as 'The Two-headed Nightingale'; Marian The Giantess '8 ft 2 ins and still growing'. Chinese dwarfs, a Chinese Giant. In 1844 the most famous midget of all time 'General Tom Thumb' was summoned to Buckingham Palace for an audience with Queen Victoria and Prince Albert, reaping publicity that helped the American showman Phineas T Barnum to earn a fortune. Joseph Merrick the 'Elephant Man' had been found in a showman's booth in East London and even when given sanctuary in The London Hospital by the Queen's Surgeon Sir Frederick Treves, he was still put on discreet display to the Victorian upper classes who were invited to 'take tea' with him.

Little wonder then that the public appetite was whetted by news of the occupant of Elmwood House – 'the sooty object with matted hair and staring eyes in a compound of Newgate, Bedlam and a Debtors' Prison.' From the warm spring of 1862 people began to arrive at Redcoat's Green in small droves. The Great Northern Railway advertised cheap weekend excursion trips to Stevenage 'to see The Hermit of Hertfordshire.' Parties disembarked – the poorer ones walked the two miles to Elmwood, the wealthier hired a carriage. One or two enterprising local traders set up weekend stalls at the entrance to the mansion and hundreds of pairs of feet began to wear a wide path across the overgrown garden to the yard at the rear of the house which the hermit's cell overlooked. That year, when Edward Copping interviewed him for *London Society,* Lucas was able to boast: 'I dare say, now, you think you see a good deal of the world, but I can tell you I see more of it than you can dream of. I have spoken here with the very highest in the land and the very lowest. They are all as one to me. I adapt my conversation to their capacity and their station. The other day I had some of the London swell mob here, and every day I have no end of tramps. I can talk slang with a thief and religion with a clergyman. I'm not afraid of talking with anyone.'

It was Copping who confirmed in print that Dickens' Mr Mopes was, in fact, a real person; alive and well and living in Hertfordshire. In his article he referred to the hermit as 'Mr L\*\*\*\*, who lives about two miles from S\*\*\*\*\*\*\*\*, a station on the Great Northern Railway in the county of Hertford.' When he visited Lucas, Copping took with him a freelance artist Waldo Sargent who provided illustrations of Lucas and Elmwood House for the magazine. His sketch 'Mr Mopes the Hermit receiving *London Society*' was the first published portrait of James Lucas and – though not the most lifelike – later became the most sought-after, appearing on postcards and souvenir china until well into the 20th Century. More important, though, was that Lucas took a liking to the two men and was extraordinarily communicative on the day they called. As a result, Edward Copping achieved something of a scoop, for unlike Dickens who wrote a biased and exaggerated account, Copping was the only journalist ever to write an extensive article which faithfully records Lucas's thoughts and attitudes to life: the thoughts of a schizophrenic mind which one moment contain points of wisdom with which one would agree, and the next are completely irrational.

Having described the house and Lucas's appearance, Copping recalled the customary barrage of quick-fire questions which the hermit fired at all his callers to satisfy himself that they meant no harm. Then – 'Our conversation has begun at once in right good earnest, and it soon rises to the dignity of a set discussion upon the influence of the cheap press. The name of a popular and widely-circulated newspaper has been mentioned, and while the hermit shows that, although living out of the world, he is quite familiar with that journal, he makes no scruple of affecting to regard it with superb derision and contempt. Indeed, he expresses his opinions that all newspapers are injurious rather than otherwise to the mass of the people, whom they mislead rather than guide. Their invariable result, it would seem, is to excite evil passions, to set class against class, to create discontent in the hearts of the poor, and to disturb the minds of the uneducated. Their proprietors are mercenary; their writers are without principle; they give expression to sentiments they condemn; they declaim against opinions they applaud.

'Then the hermit maintains that the great mass of the population, thanks to unjust laws and bad government, are far worse off than they were a couple of centuries ago; that there has been no real progress, except perhaps in medicine, during the last two hundred years; that railways are a delusion; popular enlightenment the merest humbug – he has by this time become emphatic – and sanitary reform a sham. Plagues and sweating sickness no longer prevail, he admits, but their place has been taken by new and equally fatal diseases, in spite of the Commissioners of the Board of Health. Then, too, he maintains, snapping his fingers at statistics as distorted and unreliable, that the average rate of mortality is higher than it was even a hundred years ago.

'And it now becomes evident that the hermit is getting accustomed to us; that he is losing something of the hesitating nervousness which has at times been visible in his manner; and that he is not displeased with our company. In fact, he has gone so far into the vocabulary of compliment as to say that, although he is bored by some visitors, he is always pleased with the conversation of an intellectual man. As proof, perhaps, that he means this laudation to strike home, he comes forth from the obscurity in which he has been standing all this time, and seats himself upon the window sill, steadies himself by firmly clutching the iron bars, and is at last fairly face to face with us. It is impossible honestly to assert, when he is thus brought under our very eyes, that the hermit improves upon close acquaintance.

'For – there is no disguising the fact – the man is dirty, not partially or temporarily dirty, but dirty comprehensively and permanently. His hair is dirty, his scalp is dirty, his face is dirty, his hands and arms are dirty, his body and his legs are dirty, his feet are dirty; in a word, he is dirty all over. And the difficulty of ascertaining this fact is by no means great. For if in other days the hermit was so far extravagant in dress as to indulge himself in a blanket and skewer, he now – from economical motives perhaps – dispenses with the skewer, and retains the blanket alone. Now a blanket is serviceable enough in its way, and may be employed for a variety of purposes; but when it comes to be used as the substitute for an entire suit of clothes, its short-comings are at once made evident. The hermit seems to be aware of this, for he continually adjusts and re-adjusts his one garment, that it may the more effectually perform its office and fulfil the requirements of a too fastidious civilisation. But the blanket is but a blanket after all, and cannot by any amount of folding and re-folding be made to do duty as a coat, waistcoat and trousers at one and the same time.

'The hermit has evidently been stimulated by our arrival, and by the conversation – of which, of course, he has had the greatest share – and self-satisfaction now shows itself very plainly on his features. He begins to banter us in a friendly, not to say paternal manner; he cracks one or two good-humoured jokes; he laughs aloud, a lusty and full-blooded laugh. Then feeling, as it would seem, more and more sociable and convivial, he asks us if we will take a glass of wine. It is an offer he invariably makes to strangers with whom he is pleased, so we know by this sign that we are among the number. Yet we have heard so much of the state of his glasses, and have seen so much of the state of his cell, that we plead a cold and respectfully decline the honour of taking wine with him, unusual and difficult as the honour of taking wine with a hermit may be. At this point the eager air and manner of the hermit indicate his alacrity and readiness for another discussion. He evidently foresees a triumphant opportunity of cutting every inch of ground from beneath our feet, and leaving us – articles of supererogation not being his creed – not a leg to stand upon. He is particularly anxious to impress upon me that I am puffed out with intellectual pride – mentally distended by fallacy and assumption. I am at S******** for the purpose of adding to my stories of knowledge. I do not reject this piece of information – unceremoniously as it may have been flung into my wallet – but thankfully accept everything that is offered, and meekly call upon the hermit to proceed. And he does proceed! He overturns my opinions with ruthless energy, he kicks them when they are down, he pummels them with his two fists; and in a short time they are so bruised and disfigured as to be scarcely recognisable.

'For instance, when I happen to express the not very original or startling opinion that England is a free country, he laughs aloud with ineffable contempt, and declares he would rather live in a despotic country. I venture to inquire what there is in a despotism which proves so alluring to him, and he tells me it is its simplicity and efficiency. Power, instead of being in the hands of the ignorant many, is in the hands of the educated few. The highest men in the country fill the highest offices of state, and consequently the wants of the people are better provided for than they would be if left to the intelligence of the people themselves. As a natural consequence, all goes on easily; the government has no difficulty in carrying out whatever measures it may think desirable, and everybody is satisfied. He then informs me he is a Tory. Not a follower of Lord Derby and Mr Disraeli – but a Tory of the good old stamp. Then he tells me that the Tories, even when newly-formed as a party, gave a proof of their political sagacity and patriotic enlightenment by supporting the cause of King James II. As this illustration does not by any means impress me, the hermit begins an eloquent vindication of that cruelly-treated monarch. Never, it appears, was there a sovereign more magnanimous or more enlightened, more anxious to advance his country's welfare, or more intent upon furthering the cause of true religion.

'This comes upon me like a small clap of thunder, and I can only at first reply that these views are strangely opposed to those of Macaulay (the Whig politician and historian). But at the mere mention of that name, the hermit loses all patience, and bestows more abusive epithets upon the departed historian than I should care to repeat, or the readers of *London Society* to be informed of. At this I am stunned again, and when the hermit assures me that virtuous King James never broke the law, anxious as he might be to advance the interests of his religion, I allude quite timidly to his treatment of the universities, in contradiction of that statement. But the hermit tells me I may make my mind quite easy upon this point, and that I may consider all historical documents which do not prove his case to be the merest forgeries; and as I am getting cold in the feet, and feel my argumentative power growing damp and spongy, I admit I am vanquished and meekly lay down my arms.

'That I do so evidently gratifies the hermit, for it is his desire to be regarded as a conqueror over all kinds of opponents. It is easy to see, indeed, that he likes to be thought superior to the common run of mankind, and that he strives to show he has a vast amount of wisdom stowed away under his dirt and his blanket, and that though he has abandoned the world, the world cannot very well afford to abandon him. For he tells me somewhat exultingly, that he never seeks out anyone – it is his vistors who seek out him. "I have had as many as twelve thousand in one year," he adds, "and as many as two hundred and forty in one day. I counted them and made a note of the numbers." Then, too, at parting, the hermit was anxious that our interview should leave a favourable impression on my mind. "You'll admit," he said, as he offered me his index finger in exchange for my outstretched hand, "that I have fairly met every argument you have made use of, that there is a great deal to be said on both sides, and that I have given you some new ideas upon old subjects." And he affably bade me adieu.'

'One circumstance very much struck me. The hermit never attempted to defend his strange mode of existence, or to recommend its adoption by others. He said – less in answer to my questions than to my thoughts – that he was compelled to lead the life he at present leads. It was the only means he had of escaping the persecution of relatives. What magic charm there was in his blanket and dirt which enabled him to counteract the influence of those relatives he did not explain, nor did I inquire, for there was a hesitation in his manner when speaking upon this point which forcibly suggested to me the idea of insincerity. He faltered like a man who tells a story that he feels will not be believed. Whatever may be that cause, whether it be the persecution of relatives, a capricious and quarrelsome temper, some singular form of madness, or more morbid love of notoriety, the fact remains the same. Here is a man who is still young – he is scarcely middle-aged – who, if not a profound scholar, is at least well-educated; who is conversant with the habits of good society, and who can express himself in well-chosen and thoughtful language; who has a fair competence, and what was once a pleasant home, and who might take a place among his fellow-men at once dignified, honourable and useful. We find him, instead, huddled up in a blanket, grovelling in a noisome kitchen, throwing away his income upon the idle tramp or the lazy vagrant, and exhibiting himself as a curiosity to all who choose to gaze upon him. It is impossible not to feel that here are rich gifts rendered profitless, and a life that might be fruitful in results utterly running to waste. Whether the man would delude others, or is himself deluded, he is equally worthy of our pity.'

This unique and objective report by a contemporary writer was used by many publications as the basis for their obituary notices when the hermit died a few years later. The closest Edward Copping came to finding the real reason for Lucas's behaviour was suggesting 'some singular form of madness' but – although he could not have known it at the time – his record of their conversation reveals a man displaying symptoms which today would quickly be associated with paranoid schizophrenia. Lucas did not attempt to defend his way of life in the barricaded mansion because to him there was no need. It was the only possible way he could survive against the persecution by his brother. He hated 'the cheap press' because it dared to publish views which did not coincide with his own and therefore – like the genuine historical facts submitted by Copping – they were 'the merest forgeries.' In a schizophrenic mind anything which challenges a belief is rejected out of hand as a lie and a forgery.

To those who made no serious challenge to his theories, Lucas could be absolutely charming, and nowhere is this better illustrated than in the account written by the Irish lady in the *Down Recorder*. Apart from the inaccurate statement about Dickens' attempt to disguise himself, her letter shows how Lucas was capable of winning over people by adopting a smooth line of chat. The lady was apparently taken to Redcoat's Green by the daughters of the late Vicar of Hitchin, the Rev Henry Wiles, who had been involved in recovering the body of Sarah Lucas from Elmwood House 12 years earlier and who had himself died in 1856. The Irish lady's use of the word 'intimate' when describing Lucas's relationship with the late Vicar's daughters will raise a smile but should – I assume – be taken to mean that they were just good friends!

'His real name is James Lucas, Lord of the Manor and Squire, as he is mostly called. He is between five feet six inches and five feet seven inches in height and, if dressed and clean, would be a handsome man. Thousands go to see him. We went with the daughters of the late Vicar, who had been intimate with him in his best day, and sometimes go to pay him a visit. Two of our party wouldn't come to see him but walked about. We, five in number, walked up to the window, a heap of cinders outside, and a battered wooden old fence in front of it. We stood a yard from the window and one of the ladies said "Is Mr Lucas at home?" No answer. She spoke twice more, and then a very nice gentlemanly voice said, "Oh. Is there anyone there?" Then he jumped on the window seat. Such an object! Blacker than any sweep, but a pleasant voice. He spoke for some time to those he knew, and then turned and asked my husband's name, where he lived, and where he came from. I said something in fun about Tipperary being so bad, and he replied that there were very good men there, and laughed very much when I said all the bad ones had left. Then my turn came, and he asked me my name and whereabouts in Ireland. I said "17 miles from Belfast." He said: "Near Kircubbin or Portaferry?" And when I said it was just the spot he said "Oh. I have had people come to see me from Kircubbin." I said something about him reading, and he laughingly told me (which was not true, however) that he was a great dunce at school; told us the schools he had been at; and that his father paid £300 a year for him, where he got on beautifully and did nothing; he got as far as reductions in arithmetic and stuck there. I told him I could not get beyond twice two with any degree of certainty in the multiplication table, which amused him greatly.

'Then he began to poke about, and brought a bottle of wine to the window, and carefully wiped a glass on that most vile blanket, and gave it a final polish with a bit of old paper which he picked off the ground. The glass was filled and handed to me. We had all vowed we would not touch the disgusting glass, but given as it was no one could have refused it, and the other ladies insisted on my having the first washings after that fearful blanket – all of them and myself in such a state between laughing and trying to behave properly. My husband and another clergyman had made up their mind to say something spiteful about his wasted life, poor man! But they couldn't when he was so like a gentleman and behaved so kindly. He said to my husband "You're not looking well, Sir. I can plainly see it isn't your wife's fault. I know she takes good care of you." To which my husband said something pretty, and after a little while we thanked him deferentially and bade him goodbye. I have just heard from one of the ladies who lives near him that he has been asking about us, and said he liked us very much.'

The strange contrast between the squalor of his surroundings and the graciousness of his demeanour was something Lucas's casual visitors didn't always appreciate. Mad Lucas he was called, and so they came expecting to see something approaching a Wild Man of Borneo – fangs bared, snarling and shaking the bars of his den with animal fury. When the behaviour didn't match up to the image some were disappointed and tried baiting him in order to provoke the performance they wanted. The reaction wasn't always the one they'd hoped for, however, because James was capable of cutting people down to size with words alone if it suited him. Such was the case with the haughty woman from Martinique who spent some time scrutinising him in scornful silence. Lucas bid her good-afternoon but his greeting was ignored. He tried once more, and when she still didn't reply he settled down opposite her and began to return the stare. Slowly the broken spyglass was raised into place. 'Ah,' he observed in a loud clear voice. 'A little of the coolie caste I should say.' The words were sufficient to send her storming off in wrath. An elderly London society woman received similar treatment when she asked her companion pointedly: 'Does it do tricks?' Again the appraising monocle was raised into position with the withering comment: 'Now there's an old ewe dressed lamb fashion if ever I saw one.' Sometimes James adopted a shorter and more dramatic way of ridding himself of unwanted women visitors. He would rise from the cinders, walk towards the cell window and give a large theatrical yawn, at the same time allowing his blanket to fall off. One glimpse of the grubby Elmwood genitals was sufficient to send the most persistent woman scuttling for the gate.

Rougher treatment was often meted out to those men who chose to criticise the way he lived. On one occasion a rather loud American arrived with a party of women and proceeded to castigate the hermit for betraying his family 'by living on a dunghill in the cellar of his ancestral home' at which remark Lucas flew at the bars of the window screaming: 'Who are you to presume to dictate to me what I shall do or not do? I expect you're one of those cheap Colonels or Generals just over from America – and these women with you are no doubt just as cheap!' Another innocent caller set the alarm bells ringing in the hermit's head when he happened to introduce himself as 'being connected with the law.' The visitor was given no time to clarify his statement as Lucas – fearing the man was another sent by George to cause trouble – made a dart at him through the bars, seized him by the throat and came close to choking him to death. Helped by a friend the attorney eventually struggled free and fled beneath a volley of dusty, rock-hard loaves which Lucas had picked up from the floor of his cell and was hurling with amazing accuracy.

The reaction was not entirely surprising in view of the number of outsiders who did come to cause trouble. Hermit-baiting became a weekend pastime and the police had to be called on numerous occasions. By the late sixties Lucas found it necessary to employ part-time bodyguards. Most of these were Irish vagrants who – like the one who attacked him some years earlier – he allowed inside the house with him. But even they found the stench and the strange habits of their employer too much to endure and most left after only a few weeks. Then, there came a frightening episode which forced the hermit to seriously consider his safety once more. It happened one Sunday afternoon not long after closing time, when a group of young soldiers, stationed temporarily at Hitchin, tumbled out of a pub and made their way to Redcoat's Green. There were eight or ten of them according to Lucas and their noise and aggressive behaviour caused others to beat a retreat when they arrived outside the cell window. For some time they stood there shouting the hermit's name but he had seen them coming and had disappeared into the house. Having failed to rouse him the young men decided to take further steps to 'make the old Devil show himself'. Unable to get into the mansion through any of the barricaded doors they decided the only sure way of entry was through the roof. Several scrambled up the outside of the building, using the timber logs across the windows as a ladder, and some actually reached the roof where they began dislodging the tiles and throwing them down. Not a difficult task since many were already loose and falling away through lack of maintenance. James – quite convinced that George had now called in the Army to get him out of the family home – ran for his firearms and began discharging them at random through the bedroom ceilings and a window on the first floor. The noise and the grapeshot were sufficient to sober up the soldiers. Within moments they had scrambled back down the building and scuttled for the safety of the undergrowth that was steadily encroaching upon the house.

Nobody was hurt but Lucas reported the attack to Inspector Reynolds, who felt the incident sufficiently serious to report to the Home Office. They, in turn, reported the matter to the War Office, and Elmwood House was placed out-of-bounds to all military personnel. If James had frightened the soldiers, they too had frightened him, and from that time onwards, he resolved, nobody would be allowed to reach Elmwood without first being vetted by a proper guard.

# 8

## THE FINAL YEARS
### (1868–1874)

James had been in his mid-fifties when the drunken soldiers had tried to break into his mansion, and it can be said that the incident signalled the final phase of the hermit's life. For, from that time on, James ceased to be the showman hermit – the conceited and argumentative exhibitionist to whom Dickens had taken such exception – and became more a hermit of the traditional kind, a nervous recluse. He withdrew into the decaying building and the window of his kitchen cell, through which he had spoken with so many thousands of callers during the preceding 20 years, was boarded up like all the others. For the remainder of his life he spoke to people only from the comparative safety of a small window which served a landing halfway up the impressive staircase inside the house. To enable tradesmen to pass him food and drink a small pile of bricks was placed at the foot of the wall below. The damage done by the soldiery to the roof of the mansion added to the speed with which the great house was decaying. Lucas sent for a Hitchin builder, Mr Charles French, and asked him to make the roof weatherproof, but it was impossible to repair. The timbers were in an advanced stage of decay, Mr French told him, and so were the floorboards and joists in the bedrooms. Dissatisfied with this diagnosis, Lucas wrote to Mr French telling him to make 'an immense tarpauling which, with scaffold, poles and ledgers, could be made to cover the whole roof.' Mr French replied pointing out that the first high wind would bring down the tarpaulin and probably the whole house with it. He suggested building a couple of small rooms as a lean-to on the house, where the hermit could live and sleep in more comfort, but the offer was never taken up.

Lucas chose as his bodyguards two tough Irishmen, Robert Devine and Patrick Carman, who had both worked for him on occasions in the past. They were paid a regular wage to guard the premises day and night. They refused to live in the filthy house with their employer, however, so he bought them what might generously be called a mobile home – a large wooden hut, like the traditional shepherd's hut, on small metal wheels and fitted inside with wooden bunks. This was positioned near the side entrance to Elmwood and the entrance itself was sealed off so that no caller or passer-by could see inside. Devine and Carman took their work seriously. They armed themselves with cudgels and presented a daunting welcome to any unknown caller who turned up at Elmwood House hoping to meet the occupant. Now, the bodyguards demanded of them their name and business and each had to wait while enquiries were made to discover whether the hermit was prepared to see them. If not, they were sent away.

As time went by, Lucas was prepared to see fewer and fewer people. His trusted friends were still welcome and he continued to entertain them inside the mansion with liberal supplies of gin-and-water or wine. Sundays and Bank Holidays were childrens' days, when the hermit would make what came to resemble a Papal Blessing from the Vatican, as he appeared at the upper window to dispense sweets, buns and coins to the multitude below. As throughout his life he continued to enjoy the company of youngsters but no longer was he prepared to engage in slanging matches with the *hoi polloi* that came to bait him with their crude remarks. His favourite trick with them was to appear stone-like at the window staring through them for periods as long as half-an-hour and saying not a word until they either got fed up and left or were turned away by Devine and Carman. Charles Holmes recalled in *The Journal*: 'Good Fridays, Eastertide, Whitsuntide and other holidays were grand days at Redcoat's Green. Hundreds of persons would assemble at the house though the scene was not always agreeable to the sight. On Sundays, too, parents might be seen taking their families of little children to see "Jimmy Lucas" in the hope of getting some sweets for he was still wonderfully liberal with them.'

Because James was no longer easily accessible it was, perhaps, inevitable that stories and rumours should begin to spread. By many who lived around him he was considered to be little more than a slightly up-market version of the village idiot. Over the years familiarity had begun to breed contempt and 'Mr James Lucas the wealthy eccentric' had become known by all and sundry as 'Mad Lucas the Hermit'. They began to speculate about what he got up to in that big mansion during the weeks he was never seen, and it took only the slightest spark to set off a blaze of rumour. One such spark was ignited on a night in March 1870 after a tragic accident less than a mile from the hermit's home.

Two young men from Stevenage hired a carriage and pair to take them to Luton where they spent most of the evening drinking and playing billiards at the George Hotel. In the bar afterwards they picked up a couple of part-time prostitutes, Jemima Read and Martha Hughes – 'women of loose character' as they were described later in press reports. After plying them with drink the men persuaded the girls to take a ride with them back to Stevenage. Another carriage and pair was hired, driven by the coachman at The George, Samuel Chamberlain, who was told he had to take the girls back to Luton afterwards. Later that night Chamberlain found himself guiding the carriage and pair through the narrow lanes from Hitchin to Redcoat's Green. It was a bright moonlit night and he had no lights on the carriage from which – according to various witnesses woken up along the route – a great deal of noise and ribaldry was coming. That was shortly before midnight.

Two hours later, Chamberlain was making the return journey with the two women sitting beside him on the coachman's seat on top of the carriage. Having been paid off by the two men he was trying to find his way back to Luton. However, not familiar with the intricate network of lanes leading to the main road he became hopelessly lost. Approaching a point near the Stevenage–Hitchin road known as The Folly something happened to frighten the horses. They lurched forward and the carriage careered down an embankment where it overturned in a field, trapping all three beneath it. Jemima Read was killed outright, her neck broken by the carriage wheel. Martha Hughes was knocked unconscious, and Chamberlain the coachman was pinned, still alive, beneath the side of the carriage, the outside steps of the vehicle pressing against his chest. When Martha Hughes regained consciousness all she could hear were the cries of Chamberlain, being slowly crushed to death by the weight of the vehicle. It took Martha half-an-hour to struggle free and make her way back to St Ippolyts to fetch help, but by the time help arrived Chamberlain, too, was dead. As was customary in those days the bodies were taken to the nearest public building which, in this instance, happened to be The Duke of Wellington public house on Hitchin Hill. There they were laid out on a mattress on the floor of a front room normally occupied as private quarters by the landlord William Webb.

By breakfast time the following morning (a Saturday) news of the accident had spread far afield, and throughout the weekend sightseers from Luton, Hitchin, Stevenage and all the surrounding villages flocked to see the spot where the carriage had overturned. At the Duke of Wellington, where the bodies had to be kept until the inquest was over, Mr Webb decided to boost the trade of his small working-class pub by putting the bodies of Samuel Chamberlain and Jemima Read on public view. The whole distasteful episode was recorded in *The Hertfordshire Express*:

'The bodies of one of the women, a finely grown woman of 23 and of the man were taken to the Duke of Wellington Public House on Hitchin Hill.... The bodies were laid upon a mattress in the front room and presented a very shocking appearance.... A very large number of persons called at the public house on purpose to view the bodies. The Coroner (Mr Charles Times) said it was a disgraceful thing to make an exhibition of the deceased persons and ordered the doors to be fastened. The official person in charge of the case was Mr Warren the Parish Constable and his authority was not sufficient to ensure decency and order. The medical officer and the undertaker were obstructed in the performance of their unpleasant duties and even the injunctions of the coroner were openly disregarded by Mr Webb the landlord of the inn. He insisted on exhibiting the ghastly show to his customers and visitors. When a guard was set upon the door of the room, the sight-seers were admitted by a side door; and of course while this disgusting "raree-show" was going on, the public house did a roaring trade. Eventually, to put a stop to the nuisance, the Coroner ordered the side door to be nailed up; this was done but the landlord disputed the right of this interfering with his pleasure or his business; burst open the door again and so the poor battered remains of humanity were exposed to the indiscriminate gaze of the curious crowd for yet a while longer.'

Other groups of sight-seers made their way to St Ippolyts and the cottage of Edward Andrews and his family, where the survivor Martha Hughes was recovering from the shock and bruising of the accident. Because of her injuries and the fact that she was the only witness of the tragedy, the Coroner adjourned the inquest for a week to enable her to recover. By that time rumours were filling the air like locusts. People were interested – not so much in how the accident happened – but in what might have been going on beforehand. Who were the two young men in their midst who'd brought the girls back with them? What had been going on during the two hours between midnight and when the coach crashed? *The Herts Express* claimed it knew the identity of the two men but was unable to print their names because they had disappeared and therefore could not confirm it! Then, the name of 'Mad Lucas' began to be circulated. Someone claimed to have seen the carriage outside Elmwood House. The result of this was that, by the time the inquest opened, most of the local population were firmly of the view that the foursome had spent a couple of hours of late-night drinking and debauchery in the company of the hermit.

At a doctor's insistence Martha made the journey to the inquest at The Duke of Wellington in a covered fly (a light carriage with a hood that completely concealed the occupant) but once at the inn she still had to run a gauntlet of mawkish spectators before the ordeal of giving evidence. Although Charles Times, the Coroner, reminded the jury more than once that their sole task was to discover the *immediate* cause of the accident, they, too, seemed far more interested in what had been going on beforehand. During a long period of cross-examination they tried to discover from Martha the names of the two men who had picked them up in Luton. She did not know their names, nor where they lived, she said. Wasn't it true, one juror demanded to know, that one of the young gentlemen had been to visit her at the Andrews' cottage and 'offered to help her?' No. Was it not true that prior to the accident they had been drinking at the ruined home of Mad Lucas? They had stopped outside Lucas's house, she admitted, but they had not gone inside. Making it quite clear that they did not believe half of what Martha Hughes had told them, the jury returned a verdict of 'Accidental Death' on Samuel Chamberlain and Jemima Read. Martha was taken back to Luton in the covered fly, the journey paid for out of public funds, though juryman John Day remarked somewhat pointedly: 'The gentlemen who brought the young woman to Hitchin should pay her expenses – if, indeed, they are gentlemen.' As it was, the 'gentlemen' managed to retain their anonymity. Their names were never made public, even though half the population said they knew who they were and remained convinced that the young men had paid Martha a fair sum to forget their names and, indeed, most of the events that went on at Redcoat's Green in the hours prior to the accident. Some sort of hanky-panky had gone on up at Mad Lucas's that night – of that the people of North Hertfordshire were certain.

Mad Lucas, as they called him, was never certified insane, although his brother made a second attempt to obtain a certificate from the Commissioners of Lunacy in 1872. Dickens' friend and biographer John Forster had served on the Board for ten years by then and was about to retire because of ill health. One of his last tasks was to consider George Lucas's application to have James certified. In June, Forster went to Elmwood House and managed to meet the hermit whom he found 'singularly acute and without the least trace of aberration of intellect.' George's application and Forster's comments were submitted to the Lord Chancellor for consideration, and for their meeting in July the Lord Chancellor's secretary wrote to the Commissioners reporting that no order for medical examination would be made.

This last attempt by George to have his brother removed to the safety of an institution was caused more by his concern for the hermit's health. James was approaching 60 years of age and Elmwood House was leaking like a sieve and in danger of collapsing. In some of those bitterly cold winters that struck Britain during the second half of the 19th century, life for James must have been almost unbearable. Yet still he refused to alter his ways – wearing only the filthy blanket and keeping himself warm on winter nights by partly burying himself in the still-warm ashes raked out of the kitchen range onto the floor. The one 'luxury' he allowed himself was a weekly delivery of coal but his diet was as frugal as it had ever been – a loaf or two of bread a week, cheese, a few eggs and fourpennyworth of red-herrings. Three gallons of gin were delivered once a month by Passinghams of Hitchin and, as there were fewer visitors to drink it with him, he drank most of it himself. According to Patrick Carman, the bodyguard, James never touched tea, coffee or milk, although milk was delivered on occasions for the two cats the hermit had adopted to try to keep down the small army of rats that enjoyed the free run of the house.

Those of his true friends who continued to visit him never ceased to marvel at Lucas's amazingly retentive mind, at his ability to recall in accurate detail conversations that had taken place ten years earlier. Knowledge he had stored from years of reading and re-reading the many musty books that lay scattered about Elmwood; obscure books like Ward's *Errata of the Protestant Bible* or Kane's *Historical Discourse of the Mormons*. He could recite perfectly many of Sir Walter Scott's poems; he could sing Welsh songs and recite Shakespeare. He used the knowledge acquired from old medical books to give advice on treatment of illness to the tramps who still called, and from travel books he had learned sufficient to be able to discuss with visitors places he'd never seen. Yet, of the market towns of Hitchin and Stevenage, each a couple of miles away, he knew nothing. He'd set foot in Hitchin only once in his younger days, he said, although he had driven through in the family coach several times.

Towards the end Lucas's visitors became fewer, so that those who did call sometimes found it hard to get away. Charles Holmes recalled in *The Journal* his last visit to the hermit, just a few weeks before he died:

'The afternoon was bright and cheerful, and after a few miles walk through country lanes and fields, which told me as well as the numerous birds that the beautiful Spring had really come, I reached the house and after making friends with the sentinel – a very rough Irish-looking individual whose duty it was to guard the premises from the intrusion of the idle curiosity of strangers – I was led by him to the back of the house, and after his giving three knocks with his shillelagh or short stick, his master appeared at an upper staircase window. Having introduced myself as a well-known friend of former days, he agreed to let me in, and in a few minutes I could hear him thumping and hammering at the rusty bolts and bars of the back door, which at last gave way and was opened to admit me, and was soon shut and bolted again, which reminded me of the spider and the fly.

'By the light of a solitary lamp he led the way through coal cellars and pantries to his living room, which presented a dark and dreary appearance as the shutter was closed, and the room was only cheered by a bright fire burning in the grate. While I held the lamp for him he succeeded in disentangling an old chair from the top of a heap of rubbish, and after carefully wiping the years of dust from its surface, he invited me to sit down, while he reclined on a bed of ashes in front of the fire. There was no lack of conversation, which at first turned to our last meeting of years ago, and I was surprised to see how accurately he remembered the smallest incidents that had occurred and long been forgotten by me until aroused by his active mind. I felt a strange longing come over me to penetrate further into the rooms which feet had not trod for so many years, where rumour says strange sights are to be seen and sounds heard; where the things are left just as they were 25 years ago or more. Hats and coats still hanging on pegs in the hall, the pictures, many of the frames having parted from the cords that once held them on the walls, fallen down; the beds still made as if expecting to be used; the bed curtains still hanging in rags and mildew, trying to hide the strange spectacle from gaze. But my curiosity was not indulged, for the Hermit told me that he never allowed anyone to go over the house, so, of course, I did not press it.

'Varied and lengthy was his conversation upon places and things he had seen, and it afterwards turned upon anatomy and diseases of the human body, one of which – nervousness – he entered fully into, as he told me he suffered much from it himself, and so cleverly did he discourse upon the latter subject that I ventured to remark that it was a pity he had not been brought up in the medical profession. This remark elicited no reply, and it seemed as though he wished to forget his long wasted years. The time passed quickly and pleasantly in his company, and when I rose to go he begged me to remain a little longer which I fain would have done, but as the sun had sunk far down into the west, I took leave of him, little thinking I should speak with him no more.'

Those who – like Charles Holmes – met James in the final weeks of his life could not have guessed it was about to come to a sudden end. One of the last visitors to go inside the mansion was the hermit's old friend Francis Lucas, the Quaker banker who had done so much to help him sort out his complex financial affairs. The caller was concerned to discover that James was having difficulty pronouncing some of his words and he had to help him with some of the Greek and Latin quotations that normally tripped easily from his lips. 'My head has been a good one,' he said, 'but I seem to lose my memory now at times.' But the lapses of memory were not sufficiently serious to make Francis Lucas think the hermit's life was in jeopardy.

Indeed, when James made his final public appearance on Good Friday of 1874 he seemed to be in robust health. That day, as if prompted by some unseen force, hundreds of local people flocked to Redcoat's Green to gather outside the house; more than there had been for a long time. So many, that Inspector Reynolds and two constables had to be there most of the day to control the crowds. Several merchants set up stalls along the road outside and did a brisk trade in oranges, nuts and ginger beer. Reynolds estimated later that more than 200 children were taken up to the house by their parents for an audience with the hermit. Little figures dressed as for Sundays in suit or crinolette, gazing up in awe at the wild biblical benefactor that beamed down from the staircase window far above. One by one, each was lifted up onto the pile of bricks to be interviewed. The hermit had a word for all of them. Some he asked to recite a nursery rhyme or sing a song. He offered one little girl a drink of gin-and-water. 'No thank you', she replied, 'It might go to my head.' 'No danger of that', Uncle Jimmy assured her, 'This is a special brand that goes only to the heels.' All received a gift – a hot-cross bun, a few fruit drops or a small coin. 'They were all made happy,' wrote the reporter from *The Hertfordshire Express*, 'but the little girls were unquestionably the better cared for and Mr Lucas was as joyful as any of them.'

A few days later, on Thursday 17 April that joy had left him. When the bodyguards Devine and Carman went round to the mansion to collect their wages they found James in a state of extreme fear. It was a windy day and the large peartree up against the side of the big house was swaying, its branches brushing against the window shutters. With each noise the hermit would jump and stare wildly about him as if terrified that intruders were once more about to break into his fortress. He was drinking large quantities of gin. The bodyguards told him they had to go into Hitchin and asked if he needed anything. He replied 'No' and left the window. 'As he left,' Carman recalled later, 'he seemed to stagger. I think now it was the fit coming on.'

The following morning Carman was awakened by the sound of heavy knocking on the front door of Elmwood House. He rose quickly, dressed, and left the keepers' hut to find the postman who had been trying unsuccessfully to rouse the hermit in order to deliver a letter. Carman climbed over the bolted side gate and went round to the back of the house but he, too, could not make Lucas hear. Thinking the hermit was sleeping longer than usual because of his heavy drinking the night before, he took the letter from the postman and went back to his hut to make breakfast. Half an hour later he climbed the gate again and made a second attempt to rouse his employer. It was then that he heard moaning and, realising it would be futile for him to try to break into the bolted and shuttered mansion on his own, he set off for Stevenage, two miles away, to alert Inspector Reynolds and a doctor. James had suffered a stroke during the night and was lying semi-conscious and paralysed down one side of his body. His mouth was open as he groaned and gasped for breath but he could not speak. His eyes bulged wide in an expression of fear as the policeman and his helpers scrambled over the debris of the cell towards him.

What did the hermit make of the men who had battered their way into his stronghold and whose silhouettes were groping their way towards him through the dust and smoke? Could he see them at all? Did he recognise them as old friends who'd come to help him? Or did his paranoia persist beyond the cerebral haemorrhage so that he saw, instead, his brother George coming to kill him and claim Elmwood for himself? The expression in his eyes suggested the latter.

As the horse-drawn cart carried James and his rescuer into Jacob Chapman's farmyard, 200 yards down the lane from the big house, the farmer and his family were preparing a room for the hermit, and for the first time for more than 25 years his coal-black body was laid between the white sheets of a bed. They cared for him there for nearly two days, trying to sooth away painful periods of laboured breathing. Then, in that last rally when death is imminent, James Lucas appeared to regain consciousness for a moment. The words were barely audible: 'I felt it coming on. May the Lord have mercy on my soul.' At six o'clock on Sunday morning 19 April, 1874, he died.

# 9

## A HERMIT'S LEGACY

As they prepared James for the grave an uncanny transformation took place. The village women engaged to perform the last offices began to wash the crust of his hermit years away. It was as if the covering of soot and grease had preserved him from old age. His cleansed skin had the pure, white, smooth alabaster quality of a boy. His hands, the long nails trimmed, were small and delicate like those of a woman. His body was muscular and well-proportioned, making a lie of his age and of the frugal diet on which he had existed for so long. In death his face was serene, indeed, handsome; that of a distinguished and intellectual man of high birth. His hair tied back, his beard trimmed and combed out, he looked the man he should have been but for the diseased brain inside. Esther Palmer, who helped to lay him out, commented afterwards: 'A more beautiful looking corpse I never saw.' Esther and her friends each took a lock of the hermit's hair for remembrance. It was raven-black in colour and only slightly streaked with grey.

Throughout Sunday, as news of James Lucas's death spread across the district, the crowds came again to Elmwood: this time to stand in small groups to gaze and reminisce. A few – those considered by the Chapman family to have been his friends – were invited into the farmhouse to bid the hermit a silent farewell and to marvel at the transformation.

Because nobody understood the complex mental illness which had caused James to adopt his distasteful way of life, those given the task of writing his obituary could not have been expected to offer a reasonable explanation of why he had become a hermit. Yet there is an interesting contrast between the reports written in the Hertfordshire newspapers and those in 'the cheap London press,' as James had scornfully dismissed the national dailies. The county press filled column after column with a detailed account of his life which, with the many contributions submitted by readers who had known him, were written, on the whole, with affection. They reflected the genuine sense of loss of a character who – despite his extraordinary life-style – had many good points as well as bad. Fleet Street was less considerate in its appraisals. *The Telegraph*, offering a reason for the hermit's behaviour, suggested – 'The most tenable theory by which his eccentric course of life can be accounted for is that he may have been the victim of a diseased and morbid vanity; that he was destitute of any legitimate qualifications to attain the celebrity for which he yearned, and that by living in a ruinous kitchen, going all but naked, and giving away halfpence and drams to all comers, he was able to procure a cheap and easy notoriety.' The report in *The Times* was preceded by the cynical headline A DOUBTFUL LOSS. 'The hermit Lucas who lives at Redcoat's Green, between Stevenage and Hitchin, and who is doubtless known to thousands of our readers, is supposed to be dying.... On Friday last the keeper was unable to make him hear and on listening at the side door heard groans. This induced him to send for Superintendent (sic) Reynolds and the door was burst open. On the ground floor, in the room where Charles Dickens interviewed him, was found the hermit quite insensible and grovelling in the ashes on the floor. He has not regained consciousness and but little hope is entertained of his recovery. Until now the hermit has revelled in his uncleanliness with very little injury to his health. Since his removal the doors have been barred and policemen guard the premises.'

Inspector Reynolds had been obliged to put a police guard on Elmwood House because, though dead, the hermit was continuing to attract as much attention as he did when alive. Patrick Carman and Robert Devine also remained on duty to prevent sightseers and souvenir hunters from going into the house, for many could scarcely contain their curiosity to discover just what it was like inside; to what lay beyond the cell in the rest of the big house into which none had been allowed to venture since Sarah Lucas died in 1849. It was to be several more days before they could find out, because on Monday George Lucas arrived from London with William Neale, the family servant, and ordered that Elmwood should be completely sealed until after the funeral. Preparations for this were given to George Cannon, an undertaker at Wymondley, who was ordered to make an elaborate set of no less than three coffins! The first, of elm, was lined with pillows 'to provide support for all parts of the body.' The elm coffin was then placed inside one of lead and these two in turn were placed inside a larger one of oak, which was then covered with black velvet and studded with black-headed nails.

George wanted to send his wayward brother to the grave in a manner befitting the best traditions of his wealthy family but he was also extremely concerned that it should be a private affair. Realising that the late hermit's notoriety could turn the event into something approaching a national spectacle, he went to considerable trouble to ensure that details of the funeral were kept from the public. On Wednesday night, under cover of darkness, the undertakers took the hefty coffin containing the hermit by hearse from Chapman's farm to the Great Northern Railway station at Stevenage, where it was loaded onto a special van on the night goods train to King's Cross. Accompanied by William Neale, it arrived in London in the early hours of Thursday morning. At the time nobody was aware of the irony of this clandestine journey – that the late James Lucas was taking his first and only railway journey on the train they called 'The Lucas Train', whose crews those few years earlier had stopped in the Wymondley cutting to nip across the fields for an unauthorised late-night drink with the hermit! From King's Cross James was taken to his brother's house in Marylebone Road, where the coffin remained until the funeral service on Saturday morning. Even the local press appears to have been misled over the timing of the funeral, because *The Hertfordshire Express* that week reported that James had been buried on the same day that he'd been taken to London. So George succeeded in his desire to keep the event a private family occasion. Only one reporter appears to have witnessed the affair – William Pollard of *The Herts Guardian*.

From his report one wonders whether the ceremony was more private than even George had wished, for, as the cortege began the journey of several miles from Marylebone to Hackney, he was the only family mourner. Neither of James' sisters was present, nor any member of their families. Only two coaches followed the hearse; one contained the solitary figure of George, the other William Neale and two housemaids from George's London residence. Because of the long journey the glass hearse – drawn by four black horses bedecked with plumes of black feathers – was half-an-hour late arriving. Inside the church of St John-at-Hackney only half-a-dozen people were waiting to witness the Rev R Hutton Potts BA of St John's College, Cambridge, conduct the service. Then the little group followed the coffin outside again and round to the East side of the building where the Lucas tomb stands in a long row of family vaults. There the service was completed, and James was lowered down to join the remains of his parents, Philip and Sarah, his infant brother Philip and his brother-in-law and sister, the Count and Countess de Taaffe.

'The solemn ceremony was performed with the respect and quietness of a village funeral,' wrote William Pollard, 'but it is doubtful whether more than two or three of the bystanders know of the extraordinary life of him whose obsequies they were witnessing. Thus ended the last on earth of a gentleman who, in his life, excited much curiosity; who had been visited by tens of thousands of all ranks and classes – authors included – and has given employment to many pens to describe his strange house and his peculiar mode of living.'

Before the tomb was sealed the witnesses moved forward to read the inscription on the brass plate attached to the velvet-covered coffin. The medieval lettering read simply:

JAMES LUCAS ESQ.
Born 22nd December 1813
Died 19th April 1874

Final confirmation of something which nobody outside the hermit's family had ever known for certain – his precise age. 60 years and four months.

Relieved that the funeral of his outrageous brother had passed off peacefully, George returned immediately to Redcoat's Green to discover what, precisely, was left of the estate of which for 25 years he had been denied his rightful share. Most people expected to find inside Elmwood a scene reminiscent of Miss Havisham's wedding banquet in *Great Expectations*; a house where time had stood still; cobwebs and dust shrouding a home and its contents exactly as they had been the day the Mistress of Elmwood had died. Others considered the interior would be little different to the hermit's cell – a foul-smelling refuse tip. In fact, it was a combination of both. George ordered a team of workmen to begin clearing the building, giving instructions that all the rubbish and ashes were to be carefully sieved to ensure nothing of value was accidentally thrown away. Having made a quick examination himself, George allowed reporters to be taken over the mansion while the work proceeded.

Picking their way over the thick carpet of ashes and past an enormous pile of stale loaves – 'They were as black as soot and hard as bricks and it was only by their shape that one could tell they were bread at all' – the visitors were taken into the drawing room. There, indeed, were the furniture and fittings still set out in place, but nearly all were in an advanced stage of decay. A glance upwards provided the reason. There, poking crazily through the ceiling were the legs of a bed and other furniture in the room above. So badly had the roof leaked that, with every fall of rain or snow, water had poured into the house, ruining everything with which it had come into contact. In the corner of the drawing room stood the expensive grand piano on which the hermit's sister, Anna Maria, Countess de Taaffe, had entertained the family with musical soirees. To one side were several matching chairs made of rosewood and inlaid with gilt – the horsehair seats rotted and gone. At the foot of the magnificent oak staircase – generally agreed to be the only worthwhile and solid part of the building that remained – was a large tub full of rainwater. On the middle landing were the sad remains of the gifts James had bought to distribute to the children on his last Good Friday; some eggs, stale hot-cross buns, several pounds of boiled sweets and an old saucepan containing pennies and threepenny bits. By the side of these lay the shotgun, unloaded. In another corner were the fencing foils, once used by James for his drill training and for the occasional bout of fencing with friends in his cell.

Scattered everywhere were dozens of mildewed books from which the hermit had gained his knowledge over the years. *Graham's Domestic Medicine 1840*, *Chamber's Miscellany* and *Laws of Nature and Nations*. Geography books, books of poetry and many more. Paintings and family portraits lay broken on the floor. Only a few metal oil lamps and some valuable Chinese porcelain vases had survived the neglect. Upstairs, in the largest of the south-facing bedrooms, were several large chests, securely padlocked and apparently unopened since Sarah Lucas had been alive. This had been her bedroom, but the contents of the chests were never revealed to anyone outside the family, for George had them moved back to his home in London unopened. Sarah's bedroom provided the most poignant reminders of the past. James had spent much of his time in this room during his last years and it was clear that he had tried to keep it exactly as it was before his mother died. Her wash-stand was there, and on the dressing table were her hairbrush and combs and a silver hand mirror that was no longer able to reflect an image. Her petticoats and bodices still hung in the wardrobe, and the four-poster bed was neatly made with the bedspread folded back as though awaiting her return. The bedclothes disintegrated upon touch.

On Sarah's bedside table lay her favourite books of religious poetry. James, in his many controversial and contradictory statements on religion, had never denied the existence of God, and one suspects that, in private, the religious upbringing he received from his mother remained a source of comfort through the long, lonely periods of his life. Of those allowed to look over Elmwood, several remarked on one small significant thing that had happened to each of them. Each had instinctively picked up the top book of the little pile on the bedside table to examine it, and every time it was picked up it automatically fell open at the same page. That page was dog-eared and grubby and clearly had been read many, many times. Little doubt that these sentimental verses offered James appropriate comfort for the loss of his mother and his own utter loneliness:

> O Holy Saviour, Friend unseen,
> Since on thine arm thou bid'st me lean,
> Help me through life's varying scene,
> By faith to cling to thee.
>
> Far from her home, fatigued, oppressed,
> Here she has found her place of rest,
> An exile still, yet not unblessed,
> While she can cling to thee.

> Without a murmur I dismiss
> My former dreams of earthly bliss,
> My joy, my consolation this,
> Each hour to cling to thee.
>
> What though the world unfaithful prove
> And earthly friends and joys remove,
> With sure and certain hope of love
> Still would I cling to thee.
>
> Oft, when I seem to tread alone,
> Some barren waste, with thorns o'ergrown,
> Thy voice of love in gentle tone
> Whispers 'Still cling to me.'

During the following six weeks seventeen cartloads of rubbish and ashes were taken away from inside Elmwood House. The careful sieving revealed little treasure. 16 sovereigns, all minted in 1840, were found in a small basket under the ashes in a corner of the kitchen and a few more coins of gold, silver and copper found scattered about the place together amounted to the princely sum of £10 18s 4d. The hermit's cheque book was found in an old kettle, keeping company with a mouldy bloater.

However, if Elmwood yielded up little money for the treasure-hunters, it also began to make money for others. With crowds of people still turning up to look over the place, and with many Hertfordshire people anxious to have a reminder of the famous eccentric who had recently departed, local entrepreneurs began to cash in on the souvenir potential. Photographers, some from quite far away, arrived to take photographs of the mansion, which they sold either as large prints or the small *cartes-de-visite*. William Short, from Eye, near Peterborough – 'Medallist of the Royal Academy of Arts, Artist & Photographer' – sold hundreds of such prints, the most popular depicting the bodyguard Patrick Carman posing in front of the house beside an old hitching post. Mr Short also produced what he called 'a photograph portrait' of the hermit, in which he appears to have combined his talents as photographer and artist. This portrait is reckoned to be the most lifelike ever produced and it, too, sold in its hundreds. However, certain inaccuracies annoyed Mr Pollard of *The Herts Guardian*, who felt bound to expose Mr Short's handiwork as a bit of a fraud. 'A photograph portrait of Mr Lucas is sold; but it is not a genuine production. He is seen sitting inside close to the window; and the features are tolerably like; but each of the three divisions of the window has three upright bars, and there are really only two . . . and if any one can explain by what process of photography nine upright bars can be reproduced from a window where there are only six, he will confer a great benefit on modern science. The photograph is evidently a mere composition – a make-up – it certainly is not the real window.'

Other people went in for more elaborate souvenirs. Two rival dealers in china and glassware, James Parker and Henry Boardman, both of Hitchin, commissioned a wide variety of china and pottery mementoes bearing photolithographs showing James in his cell and various views of Elmwood House. Drinking mugs, shaving mugs, cream jugs, plates – even 18-piece dinner and tea services all sold well. The three principal county papers rushed out hasty biographies of the hermit, based on their own reports and on the writings of Dickens and Edward Copping. These slim booklets of only a few pages sold for between 2d and 6d a copy and one, published by Paternoster & Hales of Hitchin from reports in the *Hertfordshire Express*, sold nearly 30,000 copies and was still in demand in 1924, half a century after the hermit's death. One Mr George Cowley of Luton was moved to write 'The Hermit of Hertfordshire', a 220-line poem (with illustrations) which was published in pamphlet form and sold for one penny. Despite its turgid doggerel it ran to six editions.

At this time Dr Daniel Hack Tuke was also busy writing, though for medical rather than commercial reasons. His paper to the Medico-Psychological Association, presented four month's after Lucas's death, reached the firm conclusion that the hermit *was* suffering from a form of insanity and that the Lord Chancellor was wrong not to sign an order to have him detained. 'The condition of the Hermit of Redcoat's Green did really pass beyond the limit of eccentricity,' he told the Association. 'His emotions were perverted by disease; but while his case was primarily one of Moral Insanity – a madness of action rather than of language – a state of degraded feeling rather than intellectual incapacity – his suspicions at times took the form of a definite delusion, which our legal friends, in search of their favourite test, ought to admit to possess some weight; and here I would add that it should be carefully borne in mind that his isolation and seclusion, and neglect of his residence and dress, did not arise from the preoccupation of his thoughts in any absorbing pursuit. It arose from his diseased mental condition and the solution of the problem of his life can be found by tracing back his history to the unfavourable circumstances of his childhood, acting upon a brain in all probability predisposed to mental disease.

'I conclude this sketch by briefly referring to the question which must present itself in such cases as this, namely, whether a man who thus acts and lives ought or ought not to be interfered with? I am, of course, well aware that this could not be done merely on the ground of the neglect of his property or his mode of life, seeing that our law, unlike the Code Napoléon and that of ancient Rome, allows unthrifts and wasters of property to do as they like. But assuming that the proofs of his insanity were conclusive, would it or would it not have been desirable to place him under care? He was not dangerous to others, nor was he dangerous to himself, except in a very general sense, but might he not have benefited, and really been more comfortable, if under medical treatment and control? And meeting, as I think his case did, the requirement of the law "that there must be something which affords demonstrative proof of the incapacity of the individual to be trusted with the management of himself and his own concerns" it certainly would have saved a great deal of trouble and much loss of property had he been under the protection of the Lord Chancellor and the inspection of his Visitors. I submit that such control would have been better for the neighbourhood, better for his family, and better for the Hermit of Redcoat's Green himself.'

Despite Dr Tuke's firm views the modern psychiatrist has some sympathy with those pioneer members of the Lunacy Commission who twice rejected the family's attempts to have James put away. For he – just like his Victorian predecessors – is still confronted with the same fundamental and often agonising problem of deciding at what point he is entitled to take away the civil liberty of his patient. Those who suffer from paranoid schizophrenia are not criminals but people with a serious illness. To have to decide on the precise moment at which an illness justifies taking away the patient's freedom is no easy matter, and yet it is a dilemma which the psychiatrist has to rethink with each new patient. Had James Lucas been born a century later, however, his family would have found it much easier to get the hermit compulsorily admitted to a mental hospital. Under Section 26 of the Mental Health Act of 1959 an order could have been obtained by his brother George on the independent recommendations of only two doctors: but at the same time, unlike the 19th century when committal to an asylum was usually a permanent affair, his stay in a modern mental hospital might have been only temporary. His illness could not have been cured but it could have been treated successfully by drugs which enable doctors to control the extreme symptoms of schizophrenia and help the patient to lead a more normal life. One particular long-action drug, administered by injection once a month, somehow manages to encapsulate that part of the patient's mind in which the delusions are formed without affecting the person's normal behaviour. Rather like the pearl which an oyster forms around a piece of irritating grit, the drug seals in the foreign body but does not destroy it. Yet, as the treatment continues so the delusions become less and less insistent.

As it was, Philip and Sarah had little choice when their boy's illness became apparent in the 1830s. They could either keep him at home or have him committed to an asylum where, in those days, brutal restraint was usually the only 'treatment' available. They chose to keep him at home – a decision which in the long-run brought 25 years of disruption to a quiet corner of rural Hertfordshire and caused the eventual destruction of a large and lovely family home.

Elmwood House outlived its Squire by less than 20 years. When the legal tangle of half a life-time was eventually unravelled, George Lucas and his one surviving sister Emma Walker became owners of a property that should rightfully have been theirs since 1849. The tenancies of the estate were put on a proper legal footing but the family did nothing to restore the mansion. Robert Devine, the former bodyguard, was allowed to live there rent-free to continue as caretaker and unofficial guide to those visitors from far and wide who were still attracted by Elmwood's strange history. A few things remained to be seen – the Lucas family coach, which had been mouldering away in a leaky coach-house for more than 30 years. That went for good one summer's night when a group of itinerant Irish harvest-workers, who'd taken to sleeping in the coach, accidentally set fire to it and, in doing so, burnt down most of the outbuildings.

The house escaped and continued to survive until the death of Emma and then George in 1890. The estate then passed on to Emma's son Edward Lake Walker, who decided in 1893 that Elmwood must go for good. The mansion was carefully demolished, and in April that year the worthwhile remains were put up for auction by George Jackson and Son, the Hitchin auctioneers. 30,000 bricks, 20,000 roof tiles, oak beams, rafters, window frames and the marble and stone fireplaces that had once graced the larger rooms. Also among the lots was the shepherd's hut in which the bodyguards had lived, and a huge alarm bell which James had had installed in the house after the invasion by the drunken soldiers. The crazy wilderness that once formed the acres of formal gardens and pleasure grounds was grubbed out and burned, and the land returned to agriculture.

Edward Lake Walker was the last descendant of the Lucas family to own the Elmwood estate. When he died in 1928 it was put up for auction at the Sun Hotel, Hitchin – the auction brochure advertising 'A farm with excellent modern farm buildings, rich pastures and productive arable land of 173 acres. Also a well-grown wood, known as Lucas's Wood, well-known as a good fox covert with fine oak and other forest trees, of nearly 40 acres. Also Lower Titmore Green Farm, with farmhouse and 22 acres and ten cottages.' With the exception of one house the estate was bought by John Inns, of Stevenage, for £7,050. Since then it has been divided up and re-sold to a number of individuals.

In the field where Elmwood House stood, gigantic electricity pylons bringing power from the East Coast to the sub-station at Wymondley dwarf a stark, solitary pine tree, which is the only living survivor of the hermit's days. Across the road, the large pond with its island – which Dickens found 'in all its foulness and filth' – is now a pleasant watering hole for cattle, beside which serious fishermen crouch beneath their green umbrellas, casting a suspicious eye upon small boys with nets and jam jars. Another local farmer now occupies the house in which the hermit died but he has no stories of hermit ghosts to tell. In one place only can the apparition still be seen and that is glowering through his cell bars on the inn sign opposite. The red-brick Victorian pub was re-named 'The Hermit of Redcoats' at the end of the last century and today stands as the sole reminder that such a character ever existed. The crumbling family tomb at St John-at-Hackney, of course, bears no reference to his incredible life. Brother George made sure of that. To read the humble inscription one would imagine that James Lucas Esq., who died 19th April 1874 was a most ordinary fellow.

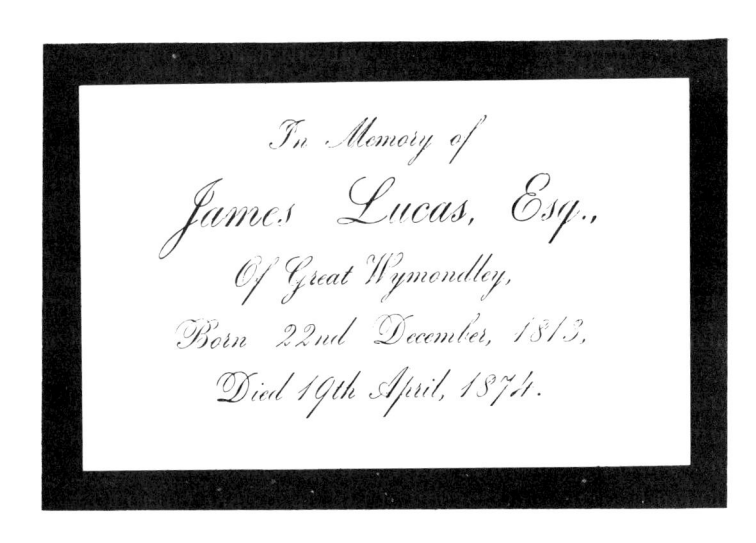

*In Memory of*
*James Lucas, Esq.,*
*Of Great Wymondley,*
*Born 22nd December, 1813,*
*Died 19th April, 1874.*

A mourning card sent out by George Lucas
to announce his brother's death.

# PEOPLE, PLACES AND MEMORABILIA

from the time of
James Lucas

The market place at Hitchin during the 1870s.

Stevenage High Street during the hermit's time, giving litt

dication that it was the main route from London to the North!

This lithograph of the hermit by William Short of Eye, near Peterborough, was considered the most life-like. Mr Short sold hundreds of *cartes-de-visite* of this picture and came in for criticism when he tried to claim it was 'a photographic portrait'.

Isaac Newton, the undertaker involved in the scandal of Lucas's dead mother.

A sketch of the Reverend Henry Wiles, the Vicar of Hitchin, who had to invoke 'the law of sepulchre' to claim the body of Sarah Lucas.

Elmwood circa 1870 showing the hermit's bodyguards Robert Devine and Patrick Carman with the mobile hut in which they lived.

A side view of Elmwood, showing its nearness to the road. Sheep hurdles had replaced the ornate iron railings that once protected the estate; only a pine tree survives today.

Fine examples of china manufactured after the death of James Lucas – from a complete commemorative tea service owned by Mr and Mrs Michael Skeggs of St Ippolyts, near Hitchin.

The view of Elmwood used for lithograph work on commemorative china.

A cheap teapot, manufactured in Germany and bearing a crude copy of Waldo Sargent's sketch of Lucas.

A sugar bowl from another tea service, using the same design.

SIXTY-FIRST THOUSAND.

# THE HERMIT OF HERTFORDSHIRE,

### BY G. COWLEY.

A true account of "a hermit of our own day,"

WITH ILLUSTRATIONS.

**PORTRAIT OF THE HERMIT LUCAS.**
(By permission of the Proprietors of "London Society").

## PRICE ONE PENNY.

The front page of George Cowley's pamphlet containing his 220-line poem on the hermit's life. More than 60,000 copies were sold. The engraving is the original by Waldo Sargent for 'London Society'.

Farmer Thomas Hailey of Little Wymondley – one of the few neighbours trusted and befriended by the hermit.

Superintendent John Reynolds, the local police chief who rescued the dying hermit from his house.

[TENTH THOUSAND].

## THE HISTORY OF
# THE HERMIT OF HERTFORDSHIRE,
CONTAINING

A Full Account of his Singular Mode of Life during Twenty-five Years of Seclusion from Society.

Re-written from the "Hertfordshire Express."

**Illustrated, in Neat Wrapper, Price 4d., by Post 4½d.**

---

**May be had of PATERNOSTER & HALES, Stationers, &c., Hitchin, and of all Booksellers in the Neighbourhood.**

An advertisement for one of the paperback pamphlets rushed out by local printers after the hermit's death.

Titmore Green Farmhouse – originally Chapman's Farm – where the hermit was taken after his rescue from the ruins of Elmwood. He died there two days later.

The author by the Lucas family tomb which he discovered on the east side of the church of St John-at-Hackney.

The church of St John-at-Hackney in East London where most of the Lucas family is buried.

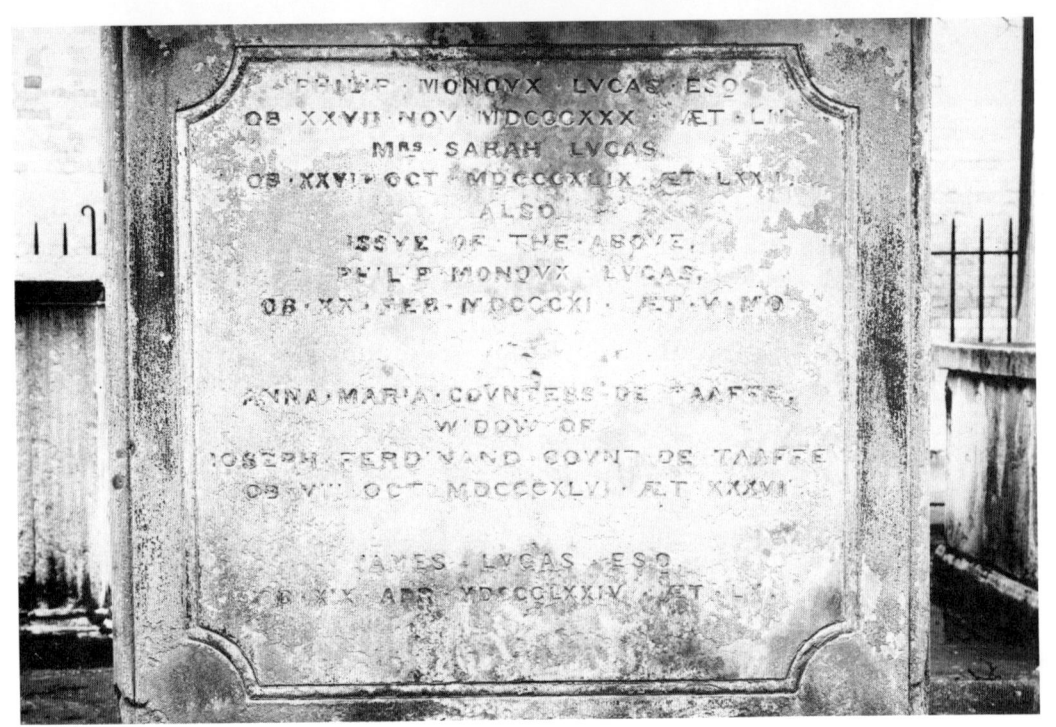

Weather-beaten inscriptions are still sufficiently clear to show the name of the hermit below those of his father and mother, infant brother and sister Anna Maria.

The 'Hermit of Redcoats' public house at Titmore Green, Little Wymondley, some 200 yards from where he lived.